THE SUCCESSFUL
CONSERVATORY

AND GROWING EXOTIC PLANTS

JOAN PHELAN

THE SUCCESSFUL CONSERVATORY

AND GROWING EXOTIC PLANTS

JOAN PHELAN

GUILD OF MASTER CRAFTSMAN PUBLICATIONS

First published 2002 by
Guild of Master Craftsman Publications Ltd,
166 High Street, Lewes,
East Sussex BN7 1XU

Reprinted 2005

ISBN 1 86108 222 3

Edited by Martin Page
Designed by Limpet Design
Drawings by Penny Brown

Typeface: Veljovic
Colour separation: Viscan Graphics (Singapore)
Printed and bound by Kyodo Printing (Singapore)
under the supervision of MRM Graphics,
Winslow, Buckinghamshire, UK

10 9 8 7 6 5 4 3 2 1

CONTENTS

ACKNOWLEDGEMENTS

I would first like to thank Vale Garden Houses of Melton Road, Harlaxton, near Grantham, Lincolnshire, NG32 1HQ who provided me with so many photographs of beautiful conservatories. They also allowed me to see all of the stages of conservatory manufacture and patiently answered my numerous queries.

I am grateful to Holloways, who allowed me to use some photographs of their conservatory furniture and to Amdega Ltd, Appeal Conservatory Blinds, Hozelock Ltd and Marston & Langinger Ltd for permission to use their photographs. Photographs were also taken at the 2001 Chelsea and Hampton Court Flower Shows. I would also like to thank the owners of the many specialist nurseries who allowed me to take photographs of their plants.

My partner in setting up Conservatory Gardens, Patricia Glennie, did so much to make it successful. Finally I must thank Andrew who not only had to wait and watch while I took photographs, but also gave invaluable help in making sure the advice in the book is clear to a non-specialist.

'Who loves a garden loves a greenhouse too'

William Cowper

The last twenty years have seen a massive increase in the number of conservatories that are being built. There is a wide range to choose from and this book aims to guide you through the process. It may be that you have already decided to build a conservatory, or perhaps you have inherited one with a new house. What will you do with it? Will it be an extra living space full of light and sun, or a place for growing exotic plants with scent and colour?

Too many conservatories are excessively hot in the summer, or too cold in winter and inhabited by a scatter of unhappy, pest-ridden plants. There is no reason why they should suffer in this way and this book will help you to find a conservatory that will fulfil you aspirations.

Once it is built you may find that you are spending more time in the conservatory than any other part of the house and it is therefore very important to get it right. The aim should be to create a structure that will give you space and comfort, yet harmonise with your house and garden. The temperature inside will be comfortable in winter and summer – both for plants and people. It will be a place where you can enjoy a successful collection of plants among your own furnishings.

One thing is certain, whether you want just a few plants or a tropical jungle you must choose species that are happy with the living conditions you offer them. The aim of this book is to make it easy for new or previously unsuccessful owners to achieve the conservatory that they dream of.

CHAPTER 1

THE
CHOICE

Why a conservatory? Why not a loft extension, a world cruise, a new kitchen or a redesigned garden? Maybe you want an agreeable place to eat and drink. Perhaps you wish for a small scale version of the Palm House at Kew Gardens. At one extreme is a Victorian fantasy with ponds, grottoes, fountains – even a few birds. At the other is an economical lean-to where the children can play. This is the stage at which you need to look at the various options that are open to you.

If you want an extra living place, possibly decorated with a few houseplants, then the conditions must favour people rather than the plants. It must be constructed to avoid searing heat in summer but be comfortably warm in winter. Here one is thinking of a garden room, possibly with a solid roof to avoid too much sun, and with insulation which will make it possible to maintain a comfortable temperature without soaring heating bills. Your success with the few plants may, however, inspire you to grow some more exotic and colourful blooms, such as bougainvillea. It is too late to realise that you need a larger, brighter conservatory. So it is important to be clear about the limitations of a garden room.

A conservatory which is suitable for a wider range of plants means providing more glass and increasing ventilation. If it is also to be used as a living space you will need to consider the needs of both plants and people. There must be room for both furniture and plants. Uncomfortable temperatures must be avoided in summer. As the balance tilts towards providing the best conditions for plants, limitations will be imposed on both the flooring and furniture. Plants prefer more humidity than people, but this creates an unfriendly atmosphere for carpets and upholstered furniture. Maintenance, particularly watering, will become more demanding. During a hot summer, watering can become a daily chore, so it is worth considering whether you want to provide borders or install an automatic watering system.

There are many choices to be made. A conservatory can be a plant house full of lush, tropical species. In an ideal world they could be provided with a hot, humid atmosphere and it could be an absorbing and rewarding project to create a replica of a rainforest. But this is not the sort of environment that most people would choose to sit in. The type and the cost of the necessary heating, together with the need to provide some form of spraying to maintain humidity would have to be carefully considered.

Previous page Fig. 1.1 Comfortable furniture and some specimen plants make a simple lean-to a welcoming extra living space. A wide doorway allows easy access to the garden.

Fig. 1.2 This wooden Victorian-style conservatory fits in well with its surroundings.

Fig. 1.3 A photograph showing the interior of the conservatory in Fig. 1.6. The space has been used to extend the kitchen and provide a dining area.

Fig.1.4 This small octagonal conservatory has a remarkable amount of space. This type of design is ideal for difficult sites.

Fig. 1.6 Lean-to conservatories can be built in the gap between buildings. This conservatory has transformed an under-utilized area of the garden into an attractive living space.

Fig.1.5 This gothic style conservatory uses underfloor heating. It is furnished with stylish cane furniture.

SITE

Most conservatories adjoin the house, either against one or two walls or as a wing. Where the house walls form part of the structure they will act as a buffer and prevent heat loss from the adjoining rooms. The walls will store heat at night but some light will obviously be lost. Of course space may be limited, but if there is a choice bear in mind the aspect, the view from the conservatory and access to other rooms in the house and to the garden. Doors opening from the sitting room or the kitchen, or better still from both, into a conservatory will make it a pleasant integral part of family life. It will be used for meals or even for the odd cup of coffee. This is less likely to happen if one has to walk from one end of the house to the other.

The size and the position of obstructions, such as trees, will affect the amount of sunlight and warmth, particularly in winter. There is also the nuisance of dead leaves in the autumn and the danger from falling branches if trees are too close. The lack of warmth can be compensated for – but there is no substitute for natural light. Exposure to wind will also affect heating bills. It is best to avoid building your conservatory between two houses because of the risk of creating a

Fig. 1.8 A simple Victorian-style conservatory has added character to this doorway.

Fig. 1.7 A lean-to conservatory with an added gable – which provides extra space and light. The doors are designed to make access easy.

Fig. 1.9 A lean-to conservatory with an added octagon allows a useful dining area to be created.

wind funnelling effect. The bigger the difference between inside and outside temperatures the higher the costs. This means that a conservatory in southern Britain tends to cost less to run than one in the north.

The amount of sunlight will, above all, be influenced by the aspect. A south-facing conservatory will receive the most sun in winter and keep your heating bills low, but you face the problem of overheating in summer. To reduce this overheating the conservatory can be built with more than one solid wall, tucked into an angle of the house or surrounded by trees to give summer shade.

A south-west- or west-facing structure will catch afternoon sun in the winter, although it is important to remember how low the sun will be in the sky and to consider whether this will affect the shade from any obstructions. This may not be ideal for a winter breakfast but it will make it much easier to avoid overheating in the summer. Blinds or other shading might only be needed on the west-facing glass and plants

would appreciate the indirect sunlight. Alternatively, a conservatory facing south-east to east will receive morning light in winter, so, if there is a choice of aspect, one should think about the time of day when the conservatory will be used. Conservatories are an ideal place to eat your breakfast during the winter and to entertain during the summer months.

A north-facing conservatory may mean little or no sun for three months of the year and even in the summer it will have less light. This limits the choice of plants. It will be more difficult to maintain a reasonable temperature in the winter, without excessive heating costs, while light-demanding plants may not grow well. On the positive side it may be more comfortable on a hot summer's day.

SIZE AND COST

If you're going to build a new conservatory, now is the time to start drawing diagrams of your house and its surroundings.

Fig. 1.10 This beautiful Victorian-style conservatory is completely in keeping with the house.

Fig. 1.11 This is the interior of the conservatory illustrated above. The central fountain and elegant palms make this an extremely attractive addition to the house.

Note anything which obstructs the sun, the paths that are needed for access and whether it will be overlooked. This will immediately mean considering the size of the building. It may be that because of the site there is only room for a small conservatory. Size also brings up the question of cost and a visit now to a garden centre or flower show will give a rough idea of the size of the structure that would fall within your price range. On the other hand, if the conservatory is too small you may always regret not paying a little more for the building that you really wanted in the first place.

The cost of the foundations and a base wall, if there is to be one, have to be added up. Decisions about the materials that are to be used in construction and accessories such as ventilation and watering systems will also influence the final outlay. Whether a conservatory will add to the value of your house will depend on the structure. A well-insulated and efficiently heated extra living space will add to the value of your house, while an unheated, single-glazed, lean-to structure will probably not.

TIME

Apart from the capital cost, heating bills may be considerable for a large conservatory and the time devoted to caring for plants will be greater. Plants in the garden can be left to fend for themselves for much of the year, but once a plant is put into the artificial world of a glasshouse you have not only the obvious job of watering, but pests and diseases are now waiting to invade an ideal environment. Dead leaves from outside plants need to be collected only once a year, but no one appreciates close ups of withered leaves and dead flowers as they relax with a drink. Tidying may take time, but it can be relaxing and an excellent antidote to stress. Be warned though;
for anyone working at home it is a very good way of wasting time, when you should be doing something else!

Glass cleaning is less appealing. It has been said that whoever in a family most wants the conservatory should be

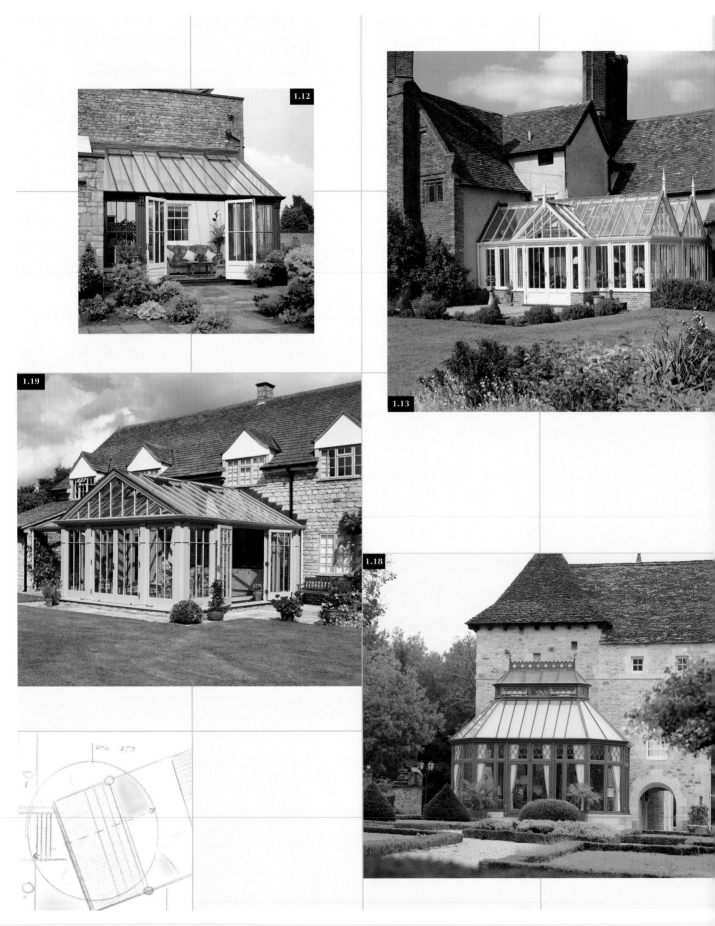

Fig. 1.12 A lean-to opening on to a patio extends the house into the garden and vice versa.

Fig. 1.13 A conservatory with a double gable.

Fig. 1.14 The interior of a first floor conservatory, which is used as a dining room.

Fig. 1.15 Exterior view of the same conservatory.

Fig. 1.16 This conservatory has intricate finials.

Fig. 1.17 This understated design makes a good foil for the house.

Fig. 1.18 An elaborate conservatory with a lantern.

Fig. 1.19 Conservatories do not have to be painted white. This wooden conservatory blends well with the mellow stone of the house.

responsible for cleaning the glass, so someone should remember this before deciding on a building which competes with the Palm House at Kew Gardens!

On the other hand it will be too late to realize the conservatory is too small once it is built. If possible visit some conservatories or at least look at photographs to see what space is required to accomodate both plants and people. Obviously any plans for using it for entertaining are relevant, as is the size of your family. If you use a round table for a dinner party with eight people it needs to have a diameter of at least 1.4 metres (5 feet). Again, an approximate scale plan may help you to reach a decision.

STYLE

Once you have chosen a site and have an approximate idea of the size it is time to think about the style of your conservatory. You want it to look like an integral part of the house; as if it has always been there. It may be that a beautiful ornate building will look best or a simple glasshouse resembling a greenhouse. The scale and proportions, the roof line, the windows, decorations and embellishments should be in keeping with the house. The choice of material – whether it should be wood or aluminium – needs consideration. The colour is also important; conservatories do not need to be white.

LEAN-TO

Perhaps a simple lean-to structure (page 7, fig. 1.6), for example, will fit the site you have chosen. The pitch of the roof and the size of the windows mirror those of the house. The use of natural-coloured wood is also in keeping and it has a wooden base wall. It has been built to extend the kitchen to make it lighter and provide a dining area. The doors lead directly on to the patio (page 4, fig. 1.3). Alternatively, a similar extension can make an attractive office, as can be seen in (fig. 1.23).

The importance of linking to the garden is shown clearly in the photograph of another lean-to conservatory (page 10, fig. 1.12), with a wide door opening on to a paved area. Three roof vents can be clearly seen. They provide good ventilation for this garden room. The colour of the wood is chosen to blend in with the plants outside. It has comfortable furniture and a few specimen plants. A gable added on to a lean-to structure can add interest and extra space (page 8, fig. 1.7). This conservatory is built on a brick base using bricks to match those of the house and adjoining wall.

OCTAGONAL

A traditional rounded or octagonal shape will suit many sites. It allows the light to come from several directions, so helping

Fig. 1.20 Ornate structures such as this beautiful Gothic-style conservatory can be rather over-powering. Here containerized plants have been used to soften the edges of the design.

Fig. 1.21 This is the interior of the conservatory shown below. It is filled with various climbing, trailing and upright plants.

Fig. 1.22 This Gothic-style conservatory complements the rather austere wall of the house.

Fig. 1.23 This conservatory is used as an office. There are no plants, but it provides a light and attractive working area.

to keep the conservatory warm. A small octagonal conservatory (page 5, fig. 1.4) can be used for plants and still have room for a table and chairs. A lean-to attached to the house can be enlarged by an octagon to give more space (page 8, fig. 1.9).

Not all conservatories need to be built at ground level. If there is little room to extend into the garden or you want to enlarge an upstairs room, they can be built onto an existing flat roof or even be supported on pillars. In fig. 1.15 (page 11) the rounded windows of the house have been copied and the ridge decorated with a crest and **finials**. It makes an attractive dining room with one solid wall – which will cut down heat loss during the winter months (page 11, fig. 1.14).

GABLED

A simple or decorated gabled or arched conservatory is often thought of as Victorian in style. They can be small, simple

Fig. 1.24 Simple wooden furniture and a variety of plants adorn this conservatory. Blinds have been used to reduce the glare from the sun.

Fig. 1.25 Extra light is provided by three raised roof lights in this large rectangular conservatory.

1.26

Fig. 1.27 This conservatory has been built with a solid roof.

Fig. 1.28 It is extremely important to make the conservatory fit in well with the house. This modern orangery has been built using brick pillars to complement the house.

Fig. 1.26 Columns between windows give a solid, classical feel to this conservatory.

structures decorated only with a finial (page 8, fig. 1.8) or be more elaborate with a porch and crest (page 9, fig. 1.10). In both of these the pitch of the roof and the style of the windows are copied from the house. There is space for furniture, a fountain, plus palms and ferns, just as in the Victorian age (page 9, fig. 1.11).

A Victorian conservatory can be made even more elaborate with the addition of a **lantern** decorated with a crest (page 10, fig. 1.18). Here the steep pitch of the roof of the house needed the extra height if the conservatory was to be in keeping with the rest of the property.

A large conservatory can often be difficult to fit in without obstructing the windows of the house and a double gable can overcome this problem (page 10, fig. 1.13). It allows you to have a steep pitch and a modest height. The roof angle is the same as that of the house but, because of the double gable, the conservatory does not dominate the house. Alternatively, a low arch can be fitted in between the windows as in the wooden conservatory in fig. 1.19 (page 10). The colour of this structure blends perfectly with the wall of the house.

GOTHIC

Gothic-style conservatories have narrow, arched windows. The decorated conservatory in fig.1.20 (page 12) complements the house. Inside (page 12, fig. 1.21), the climbers are trained over the roof, the hanging plants and potted plants make it a place suitable for both flowers and people.

Another gothic style building (page 12, fig. 1.22) shows how well a conservatory can harmonize with an old house. It is used as a sitting and dining room with cane furniture. The photograph shows the decorated grille above the underfloor heating pipes (page 6, fig. 1.5).

RECTANGULAR

Many houses, including some modern properties, look best with a simpler, rectangular structure, often referred to as Georgian. If it is going be used as a garden room it can be built with a solid roof (page 15, fig. 1.27), which will keep it cooler in summer and give better insulation in winter. With a glass roof, simple wooden furniture and blinds, the conservatory can be an ideal setting for a collection of plants (page 13, fig. 1.24). The windows of this conservatory have been carefully chosen to fit in with those of the house (page 11, fig. 1.17).

Another solution to the problem of fitting in a conservatory without obstructing the windows is to have one or more raised roof lights. They dramatically increase the amount of light that reaches the interior (page 13, fig. 1.25). Where it is appropriate, Georgian conservatories can be made to look more solid by the use of columns (page 14, fig. 1.26) or brick piers (page 15, fig. 1.28) to create a modern orangery.

CHAPTER 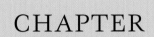 2

BRASS TACKS

T he first step in building a conservatory is putting in the foundations – which will be the same as you would need for a brick building of a similar size. There are a number of alternative structures and the depth depends on the site and soil conditions. Diagram 1 shows the type of foundation which would normally be needed. The concrete floor can either be cast on the spot or formed from slabs. Before it is laid, all the water pipes and electricity cables must be in place, so decisions must be made at an early stage about water taps and drains, heating and lighting. If there are drains running under the site they will have to be protected by a layer of concrete before the floor is laid. Any manholes within the conservatory will have to be moved or brought up to the level of the new floor and fitted with a cover, which must be airtight and watertight.

If you are going to have underfloor heating this too will need to be incorporated in the foundations. Underfloor heating requires an insulation layer, but even with other forms of heating, floor insulation should be considered as it will cut down the overall cost of heating. Remember that the concrete foundations will need at least six weeks to dry out before the floor is laid. It is essential that the foundation is perfectly level. The framework of a conservatory is not completely rigid and it is the glass which gives it strength and rigidity. If the foundation is not level the framework will be distorted and the glass may not fit.

Conservatories can either be built with the glass panels going down to the ground or resting on a base wall. Where the conservatory is to be attached to the house the decision usually depends on which will fit best with the design of the house. A base wall helps to link house and conservatory and can be made of stone, brick or wood, the latter needing to be insulated. It is worth remembering when deciding whether to have your conservatory built with a base wall, that it will help to retain heat, particularly if it is a cavity wall with an insulating layer. A cavity wall will also mean that you have a useful shelf for plant display, lamps or decorative objects, although it will cut down floor space.

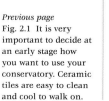

Previous page
Fig. 2.1 It is very important to decide at an early stage how you want to use your conservatory. Ceramic tiles are easy to clean and cool to walk on.

DIAGRAM 1 – FOUNDATIONS AND BASE WALL

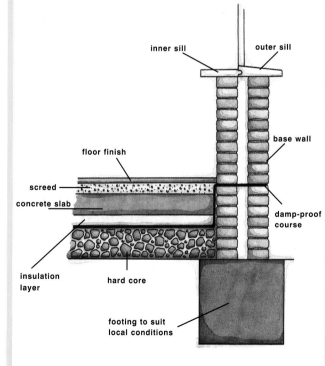

inner sill

outer sill

base wall

floor finish

screed

concrete slab

damp-proof course

insulation layer

hard core

footing to suit local conditions

PLANNING AND BUILDING

Regulations about building exist in every country, although the details of how they are applied will vary. So it is important to find out the local rules at an early stage. Failure to obtain planning permission or conform with building regulations may result in the local authority taking action against you. In the UK they have the power to issue an enforcement notice insisting that the work be reversed or remedied. If you are employing an architect or builder, or a specialist firm is erecting your conservatory they will normally deal with all planning and building regulations, but it is important to make sure this has been done. If you are building your own conservatory do get in touch with local officials to check whether planning permission will be required and what building regulations apply.

PLANNING

In the UK, development is permitted for a conservatory of up to 70 square metres although there are various provisos, such as it must not extend the original building line at the front nor interfere with the amenities of neighbours. If you are in any doubt it is wise to check with the local planning department even when it appears that the conservatory will be a permitted development. After all, a previous owner may have already used up the permitted extension.

If planning permission is necessary, application forms can be obtained from your local authority planning department or in Scotland, the local district council. There will be a small fee and it will be necessary to submit detailed plans of the development. In the case of a listed building it is always necessary to get listed building consent from the local authority but at least the work should be free of VAT. In a conservation area it would be important to check if there are any additional regulations.

BUILDING REGULATIONS

In the UK these always apply if the conservatory is over 30 square metres or is not to be built at ground level. But they can also apply to smaller conservatories in some areas. These regulations can vary widely in different areas and can be quite complex. The main points they cover are fire risk to adjoining buildings or interference with existing foundations or drains. If the conservatory adjoins the house the damp-proof course must not be covered up. An inspector will visit the site during building to check that the regulations are being obeyed and will need to see it before the concrete base is laid to check on the position of the drains, any manhole covers and the position of the house damp-proof course.

MATERIALS

The choice of materials lies between wood, aluminium and uPVC. Your decision will be influenced by the style of your house and considerations of maintenance and cost.

WOOD

Wood is always thought of as the traditional building material although, in fact, the early Victorian conservatories were built of cast iron. A wooden structure undoubtedly looks more in keeping with an older house and gives an impression of strength and solidity. It will provide a 'warmer' conservatory with less condensation, provided that the glazing system is well sealed. As it is not as strong as modern materials, the glazing bars will have to be thicker and deeper, and so will keep out more light. This may be a consideration on some sites, particularly where there are overhanging trees.

Manufacturers use different woods: the more durable softwoods such as Baltic redwood, British Columbia pine (Douglas fir) or a mahogany-type wood such as lauan or iroko. Some firms will offer you the expensive choice of oak or teak. Although it is not so strong, many manufacturers use western red cedar which is a hard softwood. It is impervious to water and therefore rotproof. It is often left unpainted and just treated with preservative as the original red colour weathers to an attractive silvery grey. The disadvantage is that it is easily damaged by the slightest scratch. Norway spruce is to be avoided as it has a shorter life. Even when the

2.2

Fig. 2.2 Wooden conservatories are more expensive than uPVC but they can be used to make a more individual building.

main structure is constructed of another wood, teak or oak may be used for the sills which are exposed to hard wear.

Whichever wood is chosen, it is important to check that it comes from a managed forest and has not been cut until it is mature. The wood must have been pressure treated with Prolin to preserve it and then been given a primer and two coats of microporous paint or stain. These paints allow for evaporation and therefore do not crack or peel. This means there is no need to strip the wood before repainting. Paints and stains are available in a range of colours and shades.

Apart from the cost, the main disadvantage of wood is the need for maintenance. Painting is obviously a time-consuming job but timber which has been properly treated should only need repainting every four years. Tackling the roof bars is the hardest part so they are often capped with aluminium. This reduces maintenance while still giving the attraction of a wooden roof inside. The capping can be supplied in different colours to match the wood. If you are planning a humid, rainforest type of conservatory, where you will be damping down the floor daily, you should be aware that there can be a danger of mildew on the wood.

ALUMINIUM

Aluminium alloys have an excellent strength to bulk ratio which means glazing bars can be thinner and they are easily extruded into different shapes – which allows conservatories to be built with curved roofs. Compared with a wooden conservatory, an aluminium structure may look 'frail' and out of place with an older house. Aluminium is a good heat conductor, so it can feel cold to touch. It is therefore important to have thermal breaks in the bars, which will prevent condensation, reduce heat loss in winter and heat gain in summer. Aluminium bars should have been powder coated and heat-treated, if this has been done they will require no maintenance. The powder coating can be done in a wide range of colours.

A successful compromise is possible if you have the roof, which is difficult to maintain, constructed from aluminium and the walls from wood. This will give you narrower and shallower glazing bars in the roof, which can be covered with a wooden moulding on the inside to match the walls.

UPVC

The plastic uPVC is, like aluminium, light and strong so the glazing bars can be thin. It is cheap, maintenance free and can be supplied in white or a 'wood' finish. uPVC conservatories are available in a wide range of different designs and can be purchased from DIY stores. While it is a very economical material to purchase it can become scuffed with time. These marks cannot be removed and, as a consequence, it cannot be recommended.

Fig. 2.3 This wooden conservatory has been painted white. This is a popular choice for modern houses.

Fig. 2.4 This uPVC conservatory has circular section drainage pipes, while the one above has square. It is worth talking to the designer and decide which you prefer.

Fig. 2.5 Aluminium conservatories are competitively priced and can look very attractive. This one has been made out of powder coated aluminium sections.

GUTTERS AND DOWNPIPES

Ordinary gutters are not suitable for a conservatory as they need to be rigid. The gutters and downpipes can be made of plastic or extruded aluminium and they can be rounded, square or the Victorian **ogee** shape, whichever looks best with the design. They can be attached by stainless steel screws or decorative brackets. Where the roof slopes down to a brick or masonry wall there needs to be a box gutter which can be concealed by a frieze.

It is a good idea to ensure that there is suitable provision for getting rid of the drainage water from the roof. A soak-away will be sufficient if there is not a convenient drain. If some of the water can be collected in a water butt you will have rainwater for watering.

FITTING TO EXISTING WALLS

Where the edge of the roof joins the main house, it is essential to have good quality lead flashings. These should be watertight and unobtrusive.

Whichever material is chosen, thought must be given to the strength of the structure. A glass roof is heavy and may have to withstand high winds and deep falls of snow. Some manufacturers incorporate steel ladder beams in the roof of the conservatory, while others use tie-bars or internal beams. Read the plans with this in mind and ask the company that is installing the conservatory what will give the essential rigidity to the structure.

GLAZING

Here the choice lies between glass and polycarbonate. Polycarbonate is cheaper and lighter, provides good insulation and diffuses the sun's rays, thus cutting down glare. Nevertheless most manufacturers use glass. The lack of clarity is the major drawback to polycarbonate as it gradually becomes cloudy, but it is also noisy when it rains and creaks on sunny days. So even if it is cheaper, do think carefully before making this choice. Try to visit a polycarbonate structure which is a few years old. Observe how the view is obscured and listen to the creaks.

In a glass conservatory regulations stipulate that safety glass must be used because of the danger of injury from any accidental damage. To retain heat, and thus reduce heating bills, double glazing is recommended. There is the added advantage that it also acts as a noise shield. Insulation starts when the gap between the panes is 6mm ($\frac{1}{4}$in) and the effect increases up to a 20mm ($\frac{3}{4}$in) gap. The problem with panes with the widest gap is that they are very heavy and require a much more substantial structure, as a result most conservato-

ries are built with 6–16mm ($\frac{1}{4}$–$\frac{5}{8}$in) gaps. Many have glass with a larger gap in the roof, because this is where the most serious heat loss occurs. A common specification is 12mm ($\frac{1}{2}$in) in the roof and 6mm ($\frac{1}{4}$in) in the walls, but in the UK the Glass and Glazing Federation recommends 16mm ($\frac{5}{8}$in) throughout. The ultimate insulation is provided by the cavity being filled with the inert gas argon.

TYPES OF GLASS

The cheapest glass is ordinary safety glass. It will fracture into small pieces if it is broken and is therefore unlikely to cause any serious injury. Toughened glass can be used; it has been heat-treated and is four or five times stronger than normal glass. It is certainly recommended for a conservatory where children may be playing. Even stronger is laminated glass, which consists of two sheets of glass with a thin transparent layer of resin sealing, binding them together. If laminated glass is broken the outer layer may break but it will stick to the resin so no pieces of glass will fly off. This reduces the risk of injury. Another advantage is that the inner layer absorbs 99.5 per cent of ultraviolet rays which cause fading of the colours in furniture and carpets – so it is worth considering for a garden room. Toughened or laminated glass also act as a burglar deterrent as they are so difficult to break through. Glass can even be made bulletproof.

All three types of glass can be constructed using low 'E' glass. This is glass which has been given a metal coating, so that some of the heat being lost from the conservatory is reflected back in. It increases insulation by about a third and is worth considering for conservatories in exposed positions or those facing north – although it is more expensive.

There is also a specialized glass, Pilkington K, which usually forms the inner pane of a double glazing unit and allows less heat to escape due to a special energy-saving coating. It is claimed it makes double glazing as effective as triple glazing. It also cuts down heat absorption in summer. The advantage of this is that by avoiding excessive temperatures in summer there may be no need to fit blinds which can be expensive and often troublesome. This glass normally has a slight blue tint but there is only a minimal effect on light absorption and it is suitable for plants. If you do not like the slight blue tinge and still want to use this glass, it is available in a clear form – but at great expense.

Georgian wired glass, with a wire mesh sandwiched between the layers of glass or attached to one side for strength, can also be found in some older conservatories but it is rarely used nowadays.

Some designs, particularly for conservatories attached to older houses, may use leaded or tinted glass. The two considerations here are the added cost and the restriction of the light. Above a swimming pool, where you might want to

restrict the light, tinted glass (which is available in different colours) could be effective. To reduce the glare in a south-facing conservatory, the roof could be made from tinted glass with clear glass in the walls.

The insulating properties of glass are given by the U value; the lower the U value the better the insulation. The table on the right gives the U value for some of the different options.

JUNCTIONS

One of the most common complaints about conservatories is that they leak. Whichever material is used to construct the conservatory it will expand and contract, so efficient gaskets between the glass and the glazing bars are essential. These can be made from neoprene, rubber or PVC.

The window joints should be mortised and tenoned. The sealed units in the roof should be stepped, that is the top sheet overlaps the one underneath, to allow rain to run straight into the gutter rather than collecting on the glazing bar. You do not want to encourage the growth of moss or lichen on the roof. The critical area is the point where the conservatory joins the wall of the house.

HEATING

The first decision to be made is what temperature you want to maintain inside your conservatory. From the point of view of plants it is the minimum winter temperature which is the determining factor. You will find that conservatory plants are normally classified as suitable for frost-free, cool (7°C /45°F minimum), warm (13°C/55°F minimum) or hot (18°C/64°F minimum) conditions. You will find many exotic plants listed as suitable for cool conditions but in addition many of the plants said to require a warm conservatory will still grow well in a cool conservatory if they are kept fairly dry in winter – although they may lose their leaves.

The temperature for people depends on how much use is to be made of the conservatory during the winter. During the day, even in winter, it should warm up if there is any brightness and this will make it possible to enjoy sitting in the conservatory. However, people sitting there in the evening may want it warmer than is needed by the plants and this will affect the decision. You will need to aim at whatever temperature you find comfortable in a sitting room. This is usually in the region of 21°C (70°F).

Whichever type of heating is chosen the energy required to give the temperature you want will obviously depend on the size and surface area, aspect, the type of glazing, amount of insulation in the walls and floor and exposure to wind. It is important to consider heat retention as well as heat provi-

INSULATING PROPERTIES OF GLASS

	U VALUE
SINGLE GLAZING	5.2–5.4, depending on the thickness of the glass
DOUBLE GLAZING	3.2 with a 6mm (¼in) gap 2.7 with a 16mm (⅝in) gap
PILKINGTON K	2.6 with a 6mm (¼in) gap 1.7 with a 16mm (⅝in) gap

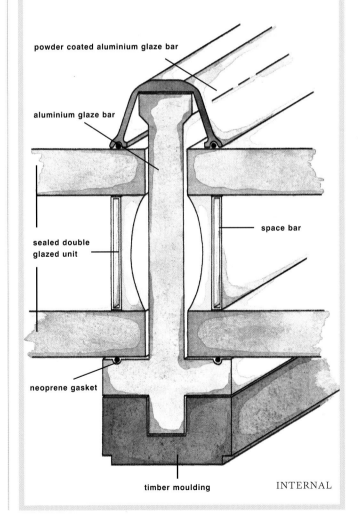

DIAGRAM 2 – CONSERVATORY ROOF EXTERNAL

powder coated aluminium glaze bar

aluminium glaze bar

space bar

sealed double glazed unit

neoprene gasket

timber moulding   INTERNAL

Fig 2.6. This aluminium conservatory has been built to enclose a swimming pool.

sion. If the conservatory is built against a house wall it will retain heat, as will the floor and base wall. An insulating layer in the floor and walls will also help to cut heating bills. While there are various formulas quoted to enable you to work out how many British thermal units will be required, it is best to rely on expert advice.

A maximum–minimum thermometer will enable you to monitor how effective your system is, particularly in maintaining the minimum night temperature in severe weather. It will alert you to the need to think of emergency measures, such as covering vulnerable plants.

UNDERFLOOR

Although costly to install, underfloor heating is not necessarily expensive to run but is clearly not an option in an existing conservatory. It also solves the problem of heating where there is no suitable wall on which to fit radiators or other fittings. Even when they can be fitted these can be unsightly unless covered by a grille, and they take up valuable space. Underfloor heating may consist of pipes fitted to

the existing conventional heating system or electric convector units installed in a trench around the edge of the conservatory under a decorative cast-iron grille. An alternative, if you would like the comfort of a warm floor, is to have small-bore pipes set in the screed under the floor tiles. These again can be heated by hot water or by electricity. Whichever method is chosen it is vital to have an effective insulation layer beneath the pipes. This type of heating is ideal for plants and very agreeable for people.

RADIATORS

A less expensive choice would be radiators heated by the house central heating. They should ideally be on a separate circuit controlled by a thermostat. This will ensure that the minimum night temperature is maintained when the house heating is switched off. It is also useful when, for example, a little early spring sun heats the conservatory and makes heating unnecessary – while it is still required in the main part of the house. Finding space for radiators can be difficult and they can affect plants near them by drying the air. If you dislike

their appearance the radiators can be concealed behind a decorative screen.

An alternative to a separate circuit, which will still maintain the minimum night temperature required when the heating is turned off at night, is electric tubular heaters on a thermostat. This does mean having to find space for both radiators and the tubular heaters. Tubular heaters can be obtrusive as they have to be at least 22cm (9in) above floor level to be effective, but this will probably be cheaper than having a separate circuit fitted.

PORTABLE ELECTRIC HEATING

Portable electric heaters are easy to install but expensive to run. Off peak rates are more economical but may not give you heat at the right time for comfort. Thermostatically controlled fan heaters are commonly used. Even if this is not the main form of heat they can be useful to provide extra heat when the conservatory is used in the evening or even during the day in winter. It is important that only models designed for damp conditions are used where there are many plants to be watered. An advantage is that in the summer, with the heat turned off, the fans can be used to keep the air moving.

AIR CONDITIONING

Keeping the conservatory cool in summer is just as important as heating it in winter. A more sophisticated but expensive choice is a heating and air conditioning unit, designed specifically for use in a conservatory. It can either be fitted into the base wall or have a separate condenser box outside. It takes up space, so it can only really be considered for a larger conservatory. You have to remember too that it means that you cannot open the windows or leave the door ajar in the summer while it is functioning.

GAS AND PARAFFIN

These are not recommended. They give off a lot of moisture and make the air very humid in the winter, resulting in condensation. They also produce fumes and there is the danger of carbon monoxide being given off, which means there must always be some ventilation to allow gases to escape. If for any reason gas has to be used it is essential that the heater is installed by a qualified engineer.

VENTILATION

When a conservatory is being constructed less thought is often given to the ventilation than heating. However, keeping cool in the summer is just as much a problem for plants and people as keeping warm in the winter. Without sufficient ventilation it may become unbearably hot, while rising humidity may also increase the danger of condensation in the evening as the air cools. The result is an increased chance of plant disease. The smaller the conservatory and the lower the roof, the greater the problem.

Blinds will help to shade the conservatory, but they are not a substitute for fresh air. With adequate ventilation it may be possible to do without or reduce the number of blinds in the conservatory. Most plants can tolerate high temperatures for a short period of time if there is good ventilation and they have enough water.

Where the conservatory adjoins a room regulations say that the total area of openings must be 5 per cent of the combined floor area. This is not adequate for the comfort of plants or people. The aim should be for a total opening area of 20 per cent of the floor area. This should include being able to open one third of the windows.

ROOF VENTILATION

Hot air rises so the most important provision is for some form of opening in the roof. Many manufacturers are reluctant to provide enough ventilation because roof openings may be unsightly and they increase the danger of leaks or draughts. However, conservatories can become extremely hot during the summer months and roof vents are the most effective way of letting excess heat escape. All plans of conservatories should therefore be carefully checked to make sure there will be enough ventilation. Once the conservatory is constructed it is difficult and expensive to remedy any shortage.

Where the conservatory has a lantern or canopy it will trap hot air and opening sashes on the sides will allow it to escape. An electric extractor fan may also be incorporated to increase the flow of air; the size of the fan will depend upon the floor area. The sashes can be controlled manually by winding handles but, as with other types of openings, the problem will be that there may be no one available during the middle of the day to open or to shut them when it rains. The answer is a thermostatically controlled automatic system. These are expensive, with the ideal system opening at a preset temperature and closing if it rains. If a lantern would not fit in with the design some manufacturers can supply an opening ridge, which is controlled in the same way.

With a lean-to structure opening vents have to be incorporated. There should be at least one for each 1.5m (5ft) and they should be capable of opening horizontally. These can also be operated manually, which will cause the same problem as before, or there are automatic vents which open by the expansion of a mineral jelly enclosed in a cylinder. Automatic vents are very useful because they can be set to open at different temperatures. However, they are not easy to adjust and you may have to climb up a ladder to reach the control. It is important to check if they are guaranteed. Automatic vents can be difficult to replace because of the

Fig. 2.7 It is essential to have enough roof vents when the conservatory is built.

Fig. 2.8 There are a wide range of electric fans available. It is important to choose one that is quiet in operation.

Fig. 2.9 Conservatories do not have to be attached to the house. This hexagonal conservatory has side windows, but none in the roof.

problem of access to the roof. The most expensive vents are controlled by electric motors and regulated by thermostats. New systems are very sophisticated and will control the size of opening and the speed of any fan which is installed.

Recently solar vents, which are powered by the sun and fitted into the roof, have come on the market. The manufacturers recommend one vent for each 12m (36ft) of floor area. It would be wise to speak to someone who has experience of these vents before installing them.

VENTILATION FROM WALLS, DOORS AND WINDOWS

The aim is to have a gentle stream of air circulating, so one needs openings that are low down in the base wall or glass to allow air to enter to replace the air rising up to the roof. If there is a base wall, ventilators with a sliding panel are very effective. For glass you need adjustable louvred panels. Ventilation from doors and opening windows is also important and it is advisable that one third of the surface can be opened if the design makes this possible.

FANS

Overhead fans can be an attractive feature and help to make the conservatory more comfortable, although they do not increase ventilation. They should obviously be fitted above head height with as much space as possible between the roof and the fan. The blades should measure approximately 105cm (3ft) across for a floor area of 13 square metres (140 square feet). If you are contemplating installing a fan, the wiring should be put in at an early stage. The movement of the air should be gentle, as plants dislike draughts. Try to hear the fan in operation before buying it, because a noisy one can be irritating.

CHAPTER

3

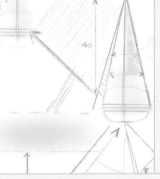

FITTING OUT
AND
FITTING IN

3.1

The floor of a conservatory matters. It is an important part of the overall image. Whatever material is chosen, it is essential to have a well-prepared base and allow it enough time to dry out. As stated earlier, once concrete has been poured in and set, it should be allowed to dry and 'cure' for at least six weeks, but another three are needed for levelling the screed (the finishing layer of mortar), if one is used. Preparation of the base will determine the quality of the floor and the stability of the whole structure. Unevenness will strain the walls and can cause major problems. Flooring must be hard-wearing and maintenance-free, because where there are plants there will be grit and the ever-present danger of spilling water.

Flooring material looks most harmonious when it is carried through from one room to another. If the conservatory is to be primarily used as a living room this can be from an adjacent room, or the patio if it is to be an extension of the garden. In a garden room a carpet will make it feel warmer, although there is a danger of it being marked by water and unevenly faded by strong light. It should be hard-wearing and water-resistant. Carpet tiles would allow one damaged part to be replaced. A covering of sea grass or sisal matting will provide a neutral background against which to display plants, and they are unaffected by water. Sea grass is a woven, natural material with a latex backing; it is hard-wearing and easy to clean as well as being economical, but note that both sea grass and sisal will shrink.

An alternative is a wooden floor. Again there is the risk of water stains, and you may find parts lightening unevenly. Properly finished wood floors are now easier to maintain but it is advisable to ask the manufacturer's advice on which wood and finish will be best if there is the possibility of high temperatures and humidity. How much maintenance will be required needs to be clarified; some finishes require only vacuuming and mopping, while others need to be re-treated periodically. Bamboo gives the warmth of wood but has exceptional stability with minimal expansion and contraction. The bamboo is treated with a plastic coating to make it stain- and water-resistant.

Tiles are the obvious choice for any conservatory where more than a few plants are to be grown. They are hard-wearing and easy to maintain, and many are weather-resistant, so they can be used on the patio, linking the two areas together. They come in a wide variety of materials: terracotta, quarry tiles, slate, ceramic, limestone or marble.

Using small or patterned tiles may look fussy and detract from the plants, particularly in a small space. Try to look at different patterns of flooring before choosing this option. Once the floor is laid you are not likely to want to change it. Patterned borders or tiles can be used as inserts to break up a large expanse of plain colour. Tiles must be non-slip when wet and have been sealed so that they do not absorb water.

Vinyl and linoleum are cheaper alternatives and are available in a range of new designs. Vinyl is sold as solid or cushioned tiles or sheets. It can mimic every other type of flooring, it is scuff- and scratch-resistant. Linoleum is prone to expansion, so is best fitted by an expert.

Stone paving slabs or concrete slabs are alternatives, particularly in a large conservatory given over to plants or where the patio outside is paved with stone. Again, by carrying through the same floor it will bring conservatory and patio together visually. If there is York stone paving outside you may like to look out for a complementary smooth York stone which has been specially prepared for indoor use. Rugs or runners in jute or coir can be used to soften a tiled or stone floor and provide texture.

Above all, whatever flooring is chosen where a whole range of plants are to be grown, rather than just a few house plants, it should be waterproof. It is difficult not to spill some water when watering in a hurry and you may wish to damp down the floor in very hot weather to raise the humidity.

Previous page Fig. 3.1
Some owners prefer the minimalist approach to planting. Here Versailles planters complement the furniture.

3.2

3.3

Fig. 3.2 This elegant
conservatory has an
English Yorkstone
floor. It is some dis-
tance from the main
house and has been
provided with its
own kitchen.

Fig. 3.3 The floor of
this conservatory is
made from limestone
with inserts of black
slate. This is a very
traditional type of
flooring and is easy
to maintain.

Fig. 3.4 Pinoleum blinds have been installed in this conservatory. Note how the elegant kentia palm softens the corner of the room.

Fig. 3.5 While the majority of the light comes from above, roller blinds can be useful for cutting out excessive brightness in the morning and evening.

SHADING

Many owners find that excessive heat in summer is a far bigger problem than cold in winter. If the conservatory has been shut up during a hot summer's day it will feel like walking into an oven. It is worth considering some form of shading if you want to avoid the soaring temperatures and glare during the summer. Shading will also help to retain heat in winter, give privacy and keep out the ultraviolet light which fades carpets and furniture.

BLINDS

These are the usual solution but they are very expensive, particularly if there are unusually shaped or curved windows. Since blinds are so expensive (up to 10-15 per cent of the cost of the conservatory), it is important to make a careful choice. Does the manufacturer give a guarantee and, if so, for how many years? How much heat would be screened out in summer

Fig. 3.6 Pinoleum blinds are attractive to look at and very efficient at reducing the amount of light that reaches the interior of a conservatory.

and how much heat-loss prevented in winter? Claims for the former vary from 33 to 90 per cent. How transparent are the blinds and will they allow enough light in for plants? Will they obstruct the view of the garden? Other points to consider are how easy are they to clean, the possibility of shrinkage or fading, mould-resistance and whether the material is flame-retardant.

Blinds can be fitted to the outside or inside of the glass. Although external blinds are clearly more effective in stopping heat before it gets in to the conservatory, they do have a number of drawbacks. They are more difficult to install and once in place they can trap leaves and other debris. They are also very hard to clean. External blinds need to be very robust because they have to contend with high winds and rain. This increases the cost. If the decision is to fit blinds on the outside there must be a 23cm (9¼in) space between the blind and the glass. Care must also be taken to ensure that there is no interference with the opening of any roof vents.

Blinds can be operated in a number of ways: manually by a system of cords, a pole with a hook or a winding handle. Obviously manual control causes problems if you are not there at the hottest time of day. You may come home to insufferable heat and wilting plants. Alternatively, they can be controlled by electric motors and a thermostat. Depending upon the design the motor may operate one blind or several. Finally, some of the computerized systems which control heating and ventilation will also control the blinds and give one a totally trouble-free but expensive time.

There are number of styles and a variety of materials. Pinoleum blinds, first used in 1860 and made from woven strips of wood, are very popular. They are durable and give an attractive dappled light. There are different weaves available which vary in the amount of light they allow through. Blinds can also be made from a variety of fabrics, many of which have a special backing which reflects the sun's rays. They can be fitted as roller or Roman blinds, the latter forming

Fig. 3.7 Mini-drippers are an ideal way of watering difficult to reach hanging baskets.

Fig. 3.8 Micro-irrigation systems can be used to water individual plants. Drippers are fed by the smaller diameter side branches.

neat folds when retracted. Many firms offer pleated blinds which they claim fit awkward geometric shapes and give an attractive effect. If shading is needed on the side windows, Venetian blinds are a good choice as they allow you to control the amount of shading by turning the louvres.

A wide range of colours exists for all types of blind, and it is even possible to have them stencilled with a pattern. Manufacturers use a range of different housings for storing the blinds when they are retracted, this should be unobtrusive and fit in with the general design. Many firms prefer to design and install the blinds themselves to ensure success, because it can be a complex process. Whoever does the installation must fit them sufficiently far from the glass to allow hot air to escape through the ventilators.

ALTERNATIVES TO BLINDS

With a glass conservatory it is possible to have a protective film applied, which, it is claimed, can reduce the temperature by up to 22°C (72°F) in summer and improves the insulation of the roof up to triple glazing standard. The advantage is that it can be used where blinds are not practicable, as on the sides of lanterns. One big advantage with this type of coating is that it requires no maintenance or cleaning, but it does not

give the flexibility of being able to open and close blinds on dull or sunny days. If you want to build a garden room it is well worth considering the option of shutters on the side windows, particularly if privacy is an issue.

Finally, although the majority of books about conservatories, and most manufacturers' brochures, suggest that blinds or other forms of shading are essential, you should look carefully at your site before you accept this advice. A south-facing conservatory with no solid walls will almost certainly need shading but a structure with a different aspect, one or two solid walls and some shading from buildings or trees, may not require any at all.

Although it may be slightly easier to install blinds at the construction stage, you may find after the experience of one summer that blinds are unnecessary or are only needed on one or two windows. Blinds are very expensive and this can result in a big saving. If, after the experience of one summer, you decide you need blinds on one or two aspects, a good firm will come and measure your conservatory and install them. It is a good idea to retain your measurements on file to make it easier to add some more blinds at a later date.

Another solution to the problem of too much heat and glare in summer is to grow a grape vine as a shade for the

Fig. 3.10 Mini-sprinklers are ideal for watering raised beds and can be easily adjusted.

Fig. 3.9 Water jets can be used to irrigate larger areas.

roof during the summer. As it loses its leaves in the winter it will allow light to penetrate during the season when it is needed. The only draw back is the fallen leaves. If light in winter is not a problem, one of the recommended evergreen climbers would be attractive.

WATERING

If you have more than a few plants to water, a tap will make the job easier and avoid water spillage when bringing water from the house. A tap with a threaded mouth, to which a hose can be attached, will help. There is no need for any internal drainage apart from the drain by the tap. Because of building regulations this must be slightly offset. Water coming from spillage or drainage from beds will not harm a tiled or stone floor and will help to maintain humidity.

If you plan to water the plants by hand nothing else is needed except for a watering can. The big advantage of hand watering is that each plant gets the right amount of water for its needs and is being regularly inspected. Any problems such as the presence of pests or disease will be picked up and can be dealt with before they become too serious. Watering in summer may well be a daily task however, so an automatic

system may have to be considered. Several firms can supply a drip feed system. The main pipe is attached to a water source and a tube with a series of little nozzles leads from it to individual plants or pots. The nozzles are adjustable to control the amount of water going to each individual plant and are able to water within a circle of 25cm (10in) diameter. If the pipe is attached to the mains a pressure reducer should be installed.

The disadvantage of this type of drip feeding is that there is no overall control on the amount of water; although a timer can be attached which can be adjusted to control the number of hours when the system will operate. However, on a hot, sunny day it may be too little and on a cool, overcast day too much. One firm does supply porous, ceramic nozzles which control the drip by losing water when the soil is dry, causing a vacuum and so opening a valve to allow water to drip through. More complex systems are controlled by a computer with temperature and humidity sensors, but this will be expensive. Even then the water will be cold and in some areas it will be hard water. If a collection of pots is being watered the tube is unsightly.

Automatic watering is easier where plants are growing in a bed. The tubes can be concealed and the water supplied from a reservoir rather than directly from the mains supply, but there will still be problems if plants which need to dry out between watering are growing beside others which prefer to be kept permanently moist. If an automatic system is being considered it is important that the pipes to provide a water source are installed at a convenient spot. The most sophisticated watering is by computer-controlled misting from overhead spray lines but this is not likely to be the solution unless you are aiming for a tropical jungle.

BEDS

Beds are often forgotten until it is too late. Providing one or more beds will give plants a real chance to grow and they look more natural than in a jumble of pots. The photograph below shows how effective a simple planting can be in a small raised bed. Climbers such as bougainvillea or mandevilla will grow faster and soon cover a wall or trellis. They are also easier to look after; especially to water.

Beds may be sunk in the floor, by leaving an area without concrete, or you can construct raised beds on the concrete base. Raised beds (see diagram) allow trailing plants to hang over the edge. Beds at floor level often look better, but it is important that they do not interfere with the foundations or the damp-proof course if they are against a wall. It can be done successfully, but builders and architects tend to raise their hands in horror at the idea. You may find you have to use a lot of pressure to introduce beds into your conservatory but you will always be grateful you succeeded. They are essential if you plan to grow more than two or three plants.

The shape of beds can vary. In a formal conservatory they often look best with straight edges, in squares, rectangles or triangles. It is best to draw outlines on a plan to see how they would look or, if you want to construct a raised bed in an existing conservatory, then chalk lines on the floor will help you to find the best design. Size will often be dictated by the design of the conservatory, but a minimum width would be 45cm (18in) plus the width of the containing wall, but think about what plants you want to grow. If you are ambitious try to aim for a larger bed.

The diagram shows the layers needed in a raised bed. It should be constructed on the scree base. The containing wall is often made of brick with a tiled coping but there is no reason it should not be constructed of other material to suit the conservatory, as long as it is strong enough to contain the soil. A waterproof layer is the first requirement; either bituminized paint or strong polythene. On top of this you need a layer of drainage material, which should be at least 10cm (4in) thick – composed of crocks or rubble with grit or sand. The soil layer can be composed of good quality topsoil or compost (John Innes No 3 is probably the most suitable), with some sand or peat mixed in to help drainage and some added organic material. The depth of the soil or compost layer should be at least 45cm (18in) and it is a good idea to incorporate some water storage granules such as vermiculite. If the decision to build the bed has been taken at an early enough stage a drainage tube can be led to the outside. Alternatively weep holes can be left in the wall.

A sunken bed will have the same layers on top of the subsoil, ie. topsoil and a drainage layer. It is advisable to double-

Fig. 3.11 If you can afford the high cost of heating, computerized misting can allow you to create your own jungle.

Fig. 3.12 Raised beds can be used as a feature in your conservatory. They can be used to grow larger, more demanding plants.

DIAGRAM 3 – A RAISED WATER FEATURE

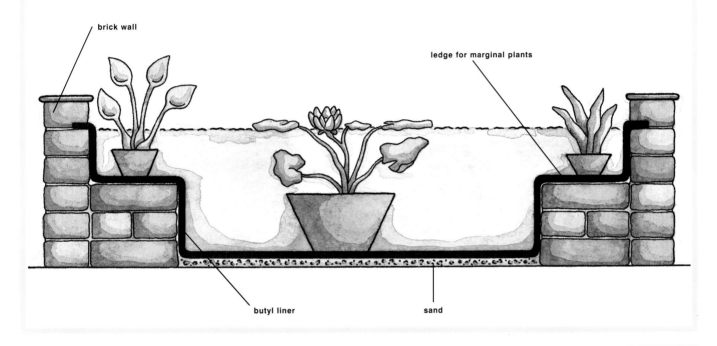

brick wall

ledge for marginal plants

butyl liner

sand

dig the subsoil first to ensure good drainage. A low wall around the bed will avoid soil spillage. If, in a garden room, the idea of possible spillage of soil is a deterrent you can still produce an effective feature by filling the bed with gravel and sinking plant pots in it.

Note that the plants benefit from being planted in a group, because the microclimate is more humid. If you bury the pots in gravel there is a big advantage in being able to move them in order to create a seasonal display.

ELECTRICITY AND WIRING

Electricity needed for the heating system is usually a priority but a power source for a backup heater – which might be needed for a winter lunch party – should also be remembered. Decisions about lighting should also be made at the planning stage. Electricity cables will have to be laid before the concrete floor and will be less obtrusive if led through the cavity walls, so do decide on the position of sockets for lighting and the layout of any heating cables. If there is no convenient socket for a lamp for reading or to spotlight an exotic plant it may mean metres of trailing flex – which is neither attractive nor safe. Draw a rough scale plan and work out where you want wall, ceiling and power outlets. Be generous, it does not cost much to add an extra socket. The frustration

DIAGRAM 4 – A RAISED BED

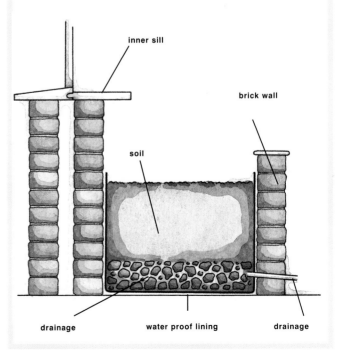

inner sill

brick wall

soil

drainage   water proof lining   drainage

of not being able to put in the wall light, to produce a perfect effect, will always be with you. You can even have a water-tight power unit in the floor for a free-standing lamp if it is planned in advance.

In an existing conservatory, any extra wiring must be carried out by a qualified electrician because of the potential danger from electricity where water is being used. This can be expensive, so thinking ahead will pay dividends. As well as the position of lights, you may need a power source for a water feature if it is going to have a pump. If there is to be a ceiling fan it will need wiring in the roof.

WATER FEATURES

A water feature can be incorporated even in a small conservatory and a pool with a calm surface, lit to reflect the plants, can transform it. A fountain on the wall, the type seen at flower shows or garden centres, will give a soothing noise of running water. The ambitious may even construct a waterfall. Moving water will need power for a pump, as has already been mentioned. A real advantage is that any water feature will provide humidity and protect the plants from the dry atmosphere – common in so many conservatories.

Ponds can be of any shape or size, they can be sunk in the ground or raised above the floor. You may decide you want the gentle noise of moving water or prefer a calm, still surface. Moving water will prevent the growth of algae. Otherwise this can be tiresome to control. A small, electric pump to keep the water moving will require a minimum depth of water of 20cm (8in), while a small water lily will need a depth of 45cm (18in). Whether sunken or raised, the pond must be constructed on a base of stable material with a layer of sand on top to avoid the liner being pierced by any sharp fragments (see the diagram on the previous page). Butyl rubber liners, used in garden ponds, will give the longest life. A sunken pool can be designed to provide a ledge for moisture-loving plants, with the liner spread over this and the edge hidden under the floor tiles. With a raised pond, which will need a low wall surrounding it, the edge of the liner can be held by the final course of bricks.

SECURITY

The main structure will be secure if it is glazed with toughened or laminated glass. These are very difficult to break through and the panels are sealed into the glazing bars. The windows and any side vents should be secure. The windows should be fitted with good locks and it is useful if they can be locked at different levels. This will allow for them to be left slightly open on hot days. If they are hung so that they open at the bottom it allows some ventilation in winter without

Fig. 3.14 It is quite common for conservatories to be an integrated part of the house. If this is the case it is essential to fit good quality locks to the doors.

draughts. Some locking devices allow the windows to be opened at the side, as well as at the top or bottom, for more ventilation in hot weather. The doors should have a mortised lock or be fitted with bolts.

The amount of space around the conservatory will determine whether doors and side opening windows are fitted to open to the outside or inside. But if you plan to use the sills for lamps, ornaments or plants, windows opening to the inside are very inconvenient.

ROOM FOR PLANTS

At the design stage of a new conservatory it is worth thinking about the sort of plants you wish to grow. What possibilities will there be for growing climbing plants? They add so much to a conservatory. A wall is ideal but they can also be trained on pillars or beams. Will there be anything from which to hang baskets? Glazing bars are not strong enough to support a hanging basket but a tie-bar or internal beam can be used. If there is a base wall, will this provide a sill wide enough for plant pots? Or would the plants look better at floor level and a wide sill merely take up valuable space? All these questions should be considered at the design stage, because you are likely to find it very expensive to change the conservatory once it has been built.

3.15

Fig. 3.13 (*far left*)
Lead is quite expen-
sive but it is capable
of producing the most
exquisite mouldings.
This lion's head forms
part of a free-standing
lead pond.

Fig. 3.15 The sound
of running water can
be very soothing after
a hard day at the
office. There is a wide
range of fountains
available from garden
centres.

4.1

CHAPTER 4

VALUE
FOR MONEY

Once you have some idea about where to site your conservatory and its style and size, it is time to look for the best way to achieve it. The site is usually determined by the shape of the house and garden, but where there is a choice, how the conservatory will be used and the effect of the aspect on the internal temperature will help you to decide on the best position. Conservatories can be free-standing, built at first floor level or even on a flat roof, as well as attached to a ground floor room in the conventional way. When you look at photographs of conservatories or visit a garden show the choice can be overwhelming. Your aim should be a conservatory which fits in so well that it looks as if it was built as part of the house.

You may have decided that you want a wooden conservatory – although it will need more maintenance – or you may prefer a lighter, more modern, aluminium structure. You may want to discuss the possibility of compromising with wooden walls and an aluminium roof. It could be that a cheap, polycarbonate structure will give you exactly what you want. Before choosing which path to follow you will have decided how much you want to spend. Remember you may see a conservatory advertized for just that amount but you have to add the cost of foundations and flooring – usually about 20 per cent of the total – and there is the further question of heating, ventilation and blinds. One thing to bear in mind is whether any existing features such as downpipes, manhole covers or boiler flues will need to be moved. Will there have to be any structural changes because of this, such as an access door to the house?

ARCHITECT

You may decide that the best way to achieve a conservatory that will complement your house and fufil your expectations will be to employ an architect. While this will be expensive you will be able to discuss with them exactly how you want to use the conservatory – an architect will look at the site with fresh eyes and may be able to suggest new ideas which had not occurred to you before.

However, architects are not necessarily specialists in this field, and it is as well to find out if they have designed any conservatories before. Are they aware of the particular problems of ventilation, shading and heating which affect this type of structure? To give you an example of what can happen, one architect designed a beautiful south-facing conservatory with glass going up from the ground to the eaves of the house. There was no ventilation in the roof or provision for blinds, so after only one summer expensive modifications had to be made. Look at the plans for your conservatory carefully. Check to ensure that there is proper provision for ventilation, for heating to maintain a minimum temperature in winter for your plants and sufficient shading if the site is south facing. If you want to incorporate beds or a pool you may have to be insistent, because some architects are reluctant to make provision for them: they will warn you about the danger of damp and may worry about building regulations. Be firm!

Once you have the detailed plans and specifications they can be sent to a number of firms asking for tenders. You may find that they want to amend the plans using their specialist knowledge to point out better ways to achieve the concept. Listen carefully to their advice, particularly if several firms are making the same point, even if your architect is not anxious to change anything. Before coming to a decision about which firm to employ you should clarify what is included in the price. Here your architect will be able to give advice. Architects will charge a fixed fee for drawing up plans, deal with any planning permission needed and ensure that the structure complies with building regulations. The architect normally supervises the actual construction.

MANUFACTURERS

You have only to look at the gardening and other press to see what an enormous number of specialist firms there are to choose from. They range from those concentrating on greenhouses – who also construct modest lean-to conservatories or garden rooms – to firms who only offer a bespoke service. Some concentrate on modern designs, others on more traditional structures.

4.2

Previous page Fig. 4.1 Flower shows are a good place to see conservatories. This impressive building was at the 2000 Chelsea Flower Show.

Fig. 4.2 Read through a range of brochures before you come to a final decision about your supplier.

4.3

Fig. 4.3 A conservatory
will provide you with
an opportunity to
grow a wide range of
attractive plants.

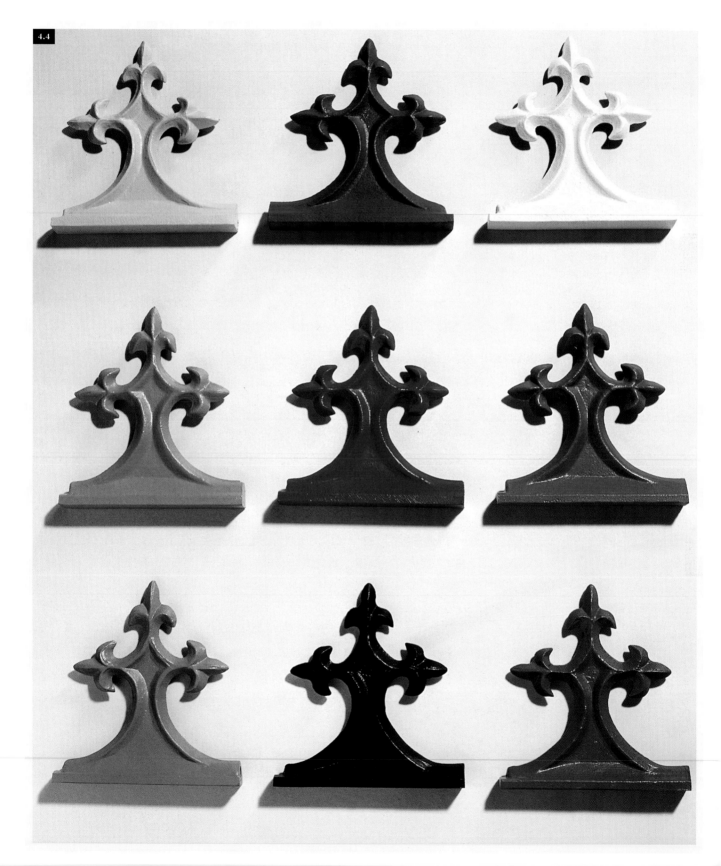

4.4

THERE ARE THREE OPTIONS:

- A ready-made design.
- A design which is constructed from a number of prefabricated modules.
- A bespoke design.

Of these the prefabricated 'ready made' design is the cheapest. Conservatories which utilise modules to fit your site are a popular option, they give flexibility at about half the cost of a completely individual design.

The first step is to send away for the manufacturers' free brochures, which illustrate their conservatories and give details of the specifications, the materials they use and the service they offer. The photographs of their conservatories will allow you to see if their styles appeal to you and may even give you fresh ideas. Never be afraid of lateral thinking: until now you may have been too conventional in your ideas.

The specifications in the brochures will suggest which firms are working to very high standards, using different hardwoods, able to match the window shape to the windows of the house or offering hand-carved finials and pediments. Their prices may well be high. Other firms will concentrate on conservatories constructed from modules, with a more restricted choice, but may still be able to give you exactly what you are looking for at a lower price. Visits to national flower shows or large garden centres will give you an opportunity to see different conservatories and talk to sales people. Some firms may be able to put you in touch with former clients. Some may invite you to visit their factory to see the actual process of construction. This is well worth doing if you have the time. Seeing the whole process of conservatory construction, from drawing up rough plans, to erecting the finished product is fascinating and may give you more new ideas. They may even have examples of different heating and ventilation systems for you to look at, in which case they can no doubt offer you advice on them.

Hopefully, after you have done all this, you will have found three or four firms which appeal to you and whose prices seem likely to come within your budget. Whether you have decided on a fixed design, prefabricated modules, or are going to ask them to design you a completely individual conservatory, the next step is to ask them to come for a site visit. You can learn a lot about each firm at this stage. Do the

Fig. 4.4 The better quality manufacturers can supply your conservatory in a range of colours. These are conservatory finials.

sales people actually walk around and look at the site, take photographs, make suggestions and listen to your ideas or do they talk hard and press their ideas? This is the time to ask the questions which will help to decide which firm will offer the best service.

- Will they do the base work and floor? If it is to be done by a builder will they recommend a firm and will they supervise the work or just provide plans?

- Will they check to see whether planning permission is required and be responsible for seeing that building regulations are complied with?

- How much of the construction is done in-house?

- Do they use their own work force to erect the conservatory or use contract labour?

- Do they show you drawings to illustrate how they give strength to the structure?

- What material do they use for the structure and, if it is hardwood, does it come from a managed forest? How has it been treated? Does the cost include final painting on site?

- If it is aluminium, is it powder coated and do they offer a range of colours?

- What type of glazing will be used? Will the roof be maintenance free?

- How much provision is there for roof ventilation? Will ventilators be automatically controlled?

- How many doors and windows are specified and how secure will they be?

- Are the costs of installing heating equipment, plumbing and wiring included?

- Does their price include door and window fittings?

- How many years' guarantee do they offer?

- What timescale would they work to?

- Are they members of the Conservatory Association (if they are based in the UK) or of a similar association which will indemnify you if the firm is unable to complete the contract?

Fig. 4.5
Conservatories need to
have opening side
windows. Make sure
that you order enough
to keep the building
cool in the summer.

Fig. 4.6 Flower shows
can be a very good
way of seeing a range
of conservatories
from different manu-
facturers.

After the discussion they will either send you rough plans
and an estimate, or they may send more detailed plans and
drawings to illustrate how the conservatory will look, with a
definite quotation. Before deciding which offer to accept and
signing a contract, take time to consider them. It is quite
common at this stage to have a delay of several months.

GARDEN CENTRE OR DIY STORE

Garden centres often sell a range of ready-made conservatories,
and their prices will probably include delivery and assembly.
While these may be remarkably good value, ask the same
questions about the type of glazing, whether the structure is
made from aluminium or uPVC and what provision there is
for installing heating. It is well worth visiting a garden centre
to see the range that is available.

If you have a reliable local builder it is worth considering
him or her for the construction work. This may be more feasible
if you are going to have a sun room built with a solid roof,
because few general builders have the experience to fit
together the modules for a conservatory roof. The glass units

are constructed so that they are strong enough for people to
walk on, but the non-expert finds this hard to believe. Be very
careful about the hard sell though, some sales people can be
very persuasive and you may not get what you expect.

DO IT YOURSELF

The final option, and of course the cheapest, is to undertake
the whole job yourself. This isn't something to consider
unless you are going to enjoy doing it, but there are firms
who provide kits ready for assembly. These mail order items
are normally simple lean-to structures
and they come complete with
instructions. The frames can be
made out of aluminium or wood,
the latter being easier to assemble.
It requires some DIY skill and it
really needs two people, although
the second person may be needed
only to hold things and to listen to
your frustrations.

The strength of the finished structure will depend to a great extent upon the exact alignment of the base and foundations and it may be worth using a builder to do this work. If the conservatory is badly constructed the first strong wind may bring disaster. A few truly skilled house owners have drawn up their own plans and built a conservatory from scratch, but they are a rarity.

CONTRACT

When you have decided which firm you want to use they will supply you with a set of working drawings. These will show you all of the details of the structure and, if you haven't already received one, they will supply you with a firm quotation. At this point you will be asked to sign a contract. It is extremely important that you check every detail of this before you sign it. You may think that the supplier understood your need for three power points and that you want brass security locks on the doors and windows – but things all too easily get overlooked. There are even horrific stories of clients not checking the measurements on the plans and find-

ing their conservatory a metre smaller than they expected. The contract will specify the terms of payment. If they require a proportion of the cost to be paid in advance you should make sure that there is an indemnity.

THE FINAL STAGE

After the months needed to make all of the decisions, building can finally start. The basework may take a little time and will usually have to be inspected by the local building inspector. Once the concrete has dried out, however, the modules will arrive ready for assembly and your conservatory will take shape as you watch. Some firms may have already assembled it in their factory to make sure all is well.

Unless you have an architect supervising the work, it is a good idea to take photographs as the work progresses in case of any dispute in the future. At the end, before parting with the final payment, turn a hose on the roof and see if it leaks. Check the entire building and make sure that you are happy with the fit of the windows, that you are satisfied with the floor and that the door locks work.

5.1

CHAPTER 5

SETTING THE SCENE

Whether you have chosen to build a brand new conservatory or to refurbish an existing one, the next step is to sit down and think about how you are going to embellish it. By now you should have decided whether you want a garden room, a dining area, a family room, or if you want to concentrate on growing a display of exotic plants.

Whatever your plans, you must first decide how much space will be needed for furniture and where it should go, remembering that you will need access from adjoining rooms and the garden. The position of plant displays will depend upon whether there is a planting bed, sills, walls or beams for climbers and on how much floor space you want to use. You must also take into account the room that is needed to take care of your plants. Bear in mind that plants grow rapidly in a heated conservatory and to make provision for the space that they will then occupy. It is a good idea to make a scale plan, showing the position of the furniture and the plants. This will help you to see how it will look when it is completed.

Decisions about the style of furniture, plant pots and stands will depend on the building. If your conservatory is built to resemble a Victorian glasshouse you may want to choose reproduction wirework furniture – complemented with pot stands in the same style. A modern, simply designed building would look better with plain, unadorned iron furniture.

It is also important to think about the colours you want to use for plants and furniture. If, for example, you are aiming for a plant display in soft pinks and mauves then bright red, patterned furniture should be avoided. A collection of spiky, green plants might well complement furniture in strong tones. A collection of Mediterranean plants would call for the type of vernacular furniture you might find in Provence.

Looking at photographs of conservatories may help you to plan your design. Visiting conservatories at a flower show may also help, even if it only shows you what pitfalls to avoid. However expensive it may be, furniture that has been chosen without considering the other components of your design will fail to produce a successful conservatory. The type of floor and the blinds, if they are to be used, needs to be considered. The plants and how they are to be displayed, the lighting and decorative features must all complement each other.

Previous page
Fig. 5.1 This wooden conservatory perfectly complements the house. The subdued lighting creates a welcoming atmosphere.

5.2

Fig. 5.3 This conservatory is decorated with old prints of vegetables and illuminated by attractive chandeliers.

Fig. 5.2 A tall yucca creates a focal point in the conservatory, with smaller plants arranged around it.

Fig. 5.4 Woven willow furniture is a good choice if you are likely to be moving the furniture around a lot.

Fig. 5.5 Rattan furniture is made from the leaves of climbing palm trees.

Fig. 5.6 Lloyd Loom furniture was first made in 1860. It is extremely attractive, and well suited to use in a conservatory.

PLANTS

Even if there are only going to be a few plants, they will determine the immediate impression of the conservatory by their shape and **habit**. If you choose bold and upright plants they will make a strong statement, whereas soft and pendulous varieties provide a gentle background. You are going to spend a lot of time surrounded by the plants so it makes good sense to choose those which you like. If you study the photographs in this book and a selection of gardening magazines, you will soon find what type of plant appeals to you.

It may be that you like the odd shapes and bright colours of **bromeliads**, the exotic flowers of orchids, or you may prefer plants which simply have beautiful foliage. If it is at all possible, try to visit a nursery which specializes in conservatory plants so you can see them growing. If you live in the United Kingdom and are unsure if there is a nursery near you, try consulting a directory such as the RHS *Plant Finder*. Specialist nurseries will have a far wider selection of tender plants than you will find in a typical garden centre. The staff are often more knowledgeable about their subject and are usually eager to share their expertise.

If there is no nursery close to you, at least send for some brochures to get an idea of prices and what is available. A visit to the glasshouses of a botanical garden is also valuable: not all the plants you see there will be available commercially, but you will get an idea of plant sizes and effective groupings.

FURNITURE

As with plants, it is better to visit a specialist firm to see the wide range of furniture that is available, than making a quick visit to a department store or garden centre. All these firms have well-illustrated brochures, so that you should be able to compare prices and see which style appeals. You will find a wide choice of materials and styles – everything from faithful reproductions to the very latest contemporary designs. The problem is deciding which will give you an ideal conservatory. Whatever style you choose, the furniture must be adapted to the conservatory environment, capable of withstanding bright light and humidity, require very little maintenance and be easy to clean.

If you see the conservatory as an extension of the house you may want to choose colours and furniture which will be

Fig. 5.7 This furniture is made from rattan and seagrass, wrapped around a bamboo frame. It is light in weight and durable.

Fig.5.8 There are a wide range of terracotta pots available. Good quality terracotta can make a major contribution to the character of a room.

welcoming in winter. If the conservatory is an extension of the garden, lighter, more summery furniture and colours which will not dominate the plants are more appropriate. However it is better not to have too much white furniture as it can be dazzling in strong sunlight – pale grey or green will look better. Whatever the type of furniture, there should be some comfortable chairs or sofas. Even in the conservatory, planned mainly as a place for growing interesting plants, you will want to sit in comfort to enjoy them or spend the evening reading in your tropical jungle.

Furniture made from cast aluminium is widely available in classic and modern styles. The paint finish, which is available in several colours, should have been baked several times to make it maintenance-free. Aluminium is light and easily moved. It will not rust and so can be moved outside to the patio or garden. Regency or early Victorian designs are also made in wrought iron, which will normally have been galvanized to prevent rusting. This may be more authentic but it is very much heavier. You may even find tables and chairs made of steel, which should be indestructible.

Wooden furniture in teak or other hardwoods is trouble-free and long-lasting – it only needs occasional treatment with oil. However, much of it has been designed for gardens,

so it may look too heavy, especially in a smaller conservatory. It does, however, have a warmer and more comfortable appearance. Softwood will be cheaper but it will need to be treated every couple of years.

For a lighter, more summery effect there is a wide choice. Rattan (made from the stems of a climbing palm tree, usually with a solid frame and woven seats and backs); wicker; willow and Lloyd Loom are all used to make chairs, tables and sofas. They are not affected by sunlight or humidity and can be kept clean by wiping with a damp cloth. The most traditional choice would be Lloyd Loom, which was first manufactured in 1860. It is made from twisted kraft paper reinforced with steel wire. It is then attached to a frame of rattan or bentwood and can be stained in a variety of colours. Chairs made from these materials can be bulky to fit around a table, so some styles of dining tables and chairs may have willow or other woven fibres on a metal frame. This gives a lighter appearance. There are also tables with glass, inlaid stone mosaic or even marble tops.

For a truly Victorian conservatory wirework is a further possibility. It has a very delicate appearance and there are reproductions of many intricate designs. When choosing cushions for your furniture, you may find it less expensive to

5.8

have cushions made locally or you may be able to find them in an ordinary furniture store. The important thing is that the material should not fade too quickly in strong light and can be washed or at least dry-cleaned. If plants are to be more than just an odd accessory the colour and pattern should be chosen to act as a foil rather than to dominate them.

POTS AND PLANTERS

Plants are usually sold in plastic pots, which are cheap, light, easy to clean and allow less evaporation than terracotta. This means less frequent watering. However, although you can find plastic pots made to look like terracotta, in general they are not so attractive. The solution might be to put them inside another pot or container and fill the space between them with peat or aggregate. This will have the extra advantage of maintaining humidity, although there is always the danger of water accumulating in the bottom. If this is overlooked it may well prove fatal for the plant. Plastic is not a good choice for large, heavy plants which need heavier pots to reduce the chance of them toppling over.

Clay or terracotta pots are attractive with their warm, orange-red colour. You can buy plain or decorated machine-

made pots, which are relatively inexpensive and come in a range of sizes and different shapes. Tall chimney pots, bowls, tulip pots or even square pots, which are easy to arrange, make it possible to find just the right pot to complement every plant. The really beautiful terracotta pots are hand-made and come from Crete, Spain and Morocco, many of them deserving to stand alone as a decoration. They are expensive but would undoubtedly make an ideal addition to the conservatory. If they are to be used for plants, avoid the **Ali Baba** pots with a narrow neck. It is hard to remove the plant without damaging it or the pot.

These clay pots have two disadvantages. Because they are porous you have to water more frequently and, in a hard water area, a deposit of lime will build up on the surface which will need to be scrubbed off periodically – unless you like the aged look. However, their appearance more than makes up for the extra work. This is particularly the case with large plants which are to stand on the floor. It is also worth looking for glazed earthenware pots from China, which come in different colours and can be plain or decorated.

All pots require saucers of some kind to collect the drainage water. There is no problem of leakage with plastic saucers but clay pots really need clay saucers which, as they

Fig. 5.9 Versailles planters are an elegant alternative to flower pots.

Fig. 5.10 The best terracotta pots are hand-made and come in a range of colours. These were made in Crete.

Fig. 5.11 Most plants need to have good drainage. This can be helped by standing the pot on feet.

Fig. 5.12 If you want to create an impact try growing the giant taro, *Alocasia macrorrhiza.*

are porous, may stain the surface. The solution is to paint the inside with clear varnish. You may prefer to use pot feet with a small china saucer under the pot – which will not be visible – to collect any water. Whichever pots you choose they must have adequate drainage.

PLANTERS

The best known planter is the square Versailles design, with round balls at each corner. They were first used in the orangery of Louis XIV. Today they are still available, made of wood like the originals, but there are also cheaper and lighter replicas in fibreglass. A Versailles planter with a citrus tree on each side of the doors will make an elegant addition to any conservatory.

Rectangular troughs in wood (which must have been treated with preservative), lead or cheaper fibreglass replicas, can be used for groups of plants which then create their own microclimate. A collection of ferns, for example, all needing the same conditions of shade and humidity, could be planted directly in the compost or left in their pots and plunged into damp peat or gravel.

PLANT DISPLAY

Some plants, often referred to as **architectural** plants, have a strong shape and can stand on their own, but most look more effective in a group. Clusters of upright plants which turn their leaves and flowers to the light look best when viewed from above. These are best placed on the floor. Pendulous plants, or those with leaves with a variegated undersurface, need to be above eye level. The one thing to avoid is having all the plants at the same height.

Étagères, or plant stands placed against the wall or in a corner, do make a wonderful display. They may be tiered or stepped and filled with plants to give a mixture of foliage and flowers. In a modern conservatory, plain styles made in anodized aluminium or rattan are cheap and sturdy, but for a Victorian conservatory there are replicas of the originals in wirework. You might even be able to find a genuine Victorian étagère in an antique shop or a cast iron plant stand with a marble top. Many of them come with trays so that pots with plants which like humid conditions can stand on damp gravel.

Fig. 5.13 Many orchids are epiphytes and they grow well if they are attached to the branch of a tree.

Fig. 5.14 Plant containers don't have to be made out of terracotta or plastic – these are woven from willow.

Fig. 5.15 Hanging baskets are useful for growing epiphytic plants.

Fig. 5.16 Étagères are a good way of presenting a range of plants in small pots.

Fig. 5.17 Wire chandeliers are a fine choice for the conservatory.

Climbing plants provide a framework in a conservatory and the more robust ones can be trained over the roof to give shade to the plants below. If there is a suitable wall horizontal wires can be fixed with vine ties. These will stand away from the wall and have a hole through which the wire can be threaded. Overhead growth can also be supported on wire but nylon tubing is less conspicuous – although it will soon be concealed. Climbing plants can also be encouraged to grow around any pillars, columns or on a trellis. Decorative trellis can be found in many different styles, oriental, **chinoiserie** or Gothic, and in many different colours. Trellis arches can also be used to create a trompe-l'oeil effect in a small conservatory and give the illusion of a plant-filled vista, as can a carefully sited mirror. A trellis closely covered with an evergreen climber can act as a living blind.

If it is not possible to support climbing plants in any of the above ways you can still add height to the display by growing them around an obelisk fitted into a large pot. A bougainvillea, for example, could be trained around an obelisk to create a pillar of colour. Evergreen climbers do well if they are grown on a moss pole.

A practical point to make is that whatever method of support is used it is important to make sure that the plants have plenty of ventilation. If they are too close to the wall or other structures there is a risk of them becoming prone to pests and diseases.

HANGING POTS AND BASKETS

Although hanging pots or baskets are too heavy to hang from glazing bars, if there is a suitable beam or rod for attaching them you have an opportunity to add more plants without taking up valuable space. They can also be hung on the wall from brackets, although they can look rather clumsy, and wall pots with trailing plants might look better. The baskets, like those on a patio, can be made of galvanized or PVC wire lined with peat. There are also terracotta hanging pots which may look better in a conservatory.

Plants displayed like this will mean more work as, being high up and exposed, they will lose water rapidly, so you will need a strategy for frequent watering. You do not want to have to fetch a step ladder every day to reach them. There are special attachments called 'Hi-Loo' with a hook allowing the pot to be pulled down and watering devices with long spouts. Watering hanging baskets can be a bit of a chore but it can be simplified by using a micro-irrigation system. These will water the plants at pre-determined times of the day.

5.18

5.19

Fig. 5.18 This griffon would make a good talking point for your conservatory.

Fig. 5.19 Classical statues will merge into the background.

MOSS TREES

If you wish to grow bromeliads or orchids, which in nature are found living on trees and absorbing water and minerals through their leaves or aerial roots, you might perhaps consider growing them on a bromeliad or orchid tree. The simplest form is to find an interestingly shaped branch and anchor it in a heavy pot or wedge it in a planting bed. To attach the plants to the branch, tie a generous layer of fresh sphagnum moss around it with plastic-covered wire. When this has been done place the plant on the tree, cover the roots with moss and tie them in place. Remember that the plants need to be misted, because they absorb water through their leaves and aerial roots.

LIGHTING

If you want to have a central light, a wire chandelier is a good choice because it won't look too heavy. But as light will be lost to the outside at night the best effect comes from low-intensity lights. Table and standard lamps or wall lights can be positioned for reading or dining. Lights shining up into a group of plants or a spotlight directed onto a favourite specimen can create a magical effect. Candles and oil lamps give a perfect soft light for a dinner party. Outside lights will allow you to look out and give you the impression of sitting in the middle of an exotic garden.

DECORATIVE FEATURES

Here you can really let your imagination take over. You can follow the Victorian tradition by having replicas of a classical statue or heads peering out from a corner of foliage plants. Or you might prefer a more modern statue or sculptures of birds or animals – such as herons at the edge of a water feature or a more modest frog peeping out from a group of pots. A group of balsawood parrots would fit in with exotic plants, or you could always have a live parrot.

A decorative urn on a plinth can be the focal point of the display. Even if a wall is covered with climbing plants they may lose their leaves in winter or need to be cut back and then wall plaques will add interest in their place. There are many traditional designs such as lion masks and gargoyles, or more contemporary ones, such as a golden Mexican sun god. Some people use a group of attractive ceramic tiles or decorative plates to decorate a wall.

One of the best ways to find something which will add the finishing touch to your conservatory is to visit a flower show where many of the sculptors will be exhibiting their work. It is also an opportunity to see furniture, pots, planters and troughs.

Fig. 5.20 Modern sculpture can be used to make a statement.

Fig. 5.21 Children are always fascinated by grotesque masks.

CHAPTER

6

TENDER
LOVING CARE

It is comforting that the majority of plants are fairly tolerant and can survive imperfect treatment. They may not grow so fast or look quite so perfect for a time but they will quickly recover with some tender, loving care. Often a few weeks outside in the garden during the summer will work miracles. Instructions may be confusing, because one authority may say that a plant needs to be fed every two weeks with half strength fertilizer, while the next advises weekly feeds using full strength. The fact is it will not matter, everyone works out their own good practice.

CHOOSING PLANTS

The most important decisions are made when plants are being purchased. If they have had a really poor start in life they will take time to recover and during that time they will not only look unhappy but will be more susceptible to pests and diseases. If a plant has been allowed to grow leggy or droopy it can be very hard to improve the shape. The plant to choose will look vigorous with a good leaf colour and will have no holes or blotches on the leaves. It is important to look carefully at the shoot tips and undersurface of leaves, because this is where any pests will be lurking. Discard any plants which are loose in their pot. This means they have not grown since they were last repotted. Discard any pots with a mass of weeds on the surface of the compost or with roots coming out of the bottom of the pot. This indicates they have been left in the pot too long. Once growth has been checked in this way it may be some time before it will get going again.

The compost should be moist. If it is dry on top, push a finger below the surface to check it is moist below the surface. At all costs avoid any pot which is waterlogged or where the compost is smelly, the roots are unlikely to recover from this treatment. One aspect of growing plants in a conservatory is that they grow so fast compared to plants in the garden that one can afford to buy young plants which will be cheaper and less likely to have been exposed to poor conditions. If plants come from friends, tact may be required if you are offered an aphid-infested specimen. Wherever they come from, it is always wise to isolate new plants for a week or so. Pests and disease can spread very rapidly.

Lastly, great care is needed on the journey home, particularly in winter. Even a few hours in the draughty boot of a car without protection can cause a lot of harm. Mail order is best confined to the warmer months and good nurseries will normally only send tender plants in spring or summer.

Once home, keep them in similar conditions to those from which they came and allow them to adapt slowly. If, for example, they were sitting in direct sun in a nursery give them as much light as you can to begin with and then gradually move them into more shade, if that it is to be their final position.

Previous page
Fig. 6.1 Ferns need shading and humid conditions to grow well.

Fig. 6.2 When you're buying plants for your conservatory make sure that they are in good condition.

PLANT NEEDS

Plants all need light, air to provide carbon dioxide for growth, oxygen for respiration, a suitable temperature, water and some **essential minerals**. Most plants have to be grown in a medium which offers some support and several, such as climbers, may need additional support.

The amount of light, water, minerals and the best temperature for growth will depend on where a plant comes from, so knowing the origin of any plant you buy will give an idea of the conditions it likes. Mediterranean plants will have adapted to a cold, wet winter and a hot, dry summer with lots of sun. These plants will appreciate a winter rest and tolerate

LIGHT

All green plants need light as the source of energy for **photosynthesis**. The light is absorbed by the chlorophyll which gives them their green colour, so variegated plants with less green colour will generally need more light. In the northern hemisphere, where winter days are short, as much light as possible will be needed, which means that the glass of the conservatory and the plant leaves should be kept clean.

Too little light is less damaging than too much but it can produce weak, spindly plants which bend towards what light there is. Too much light, however, can damage the leaves by scorching them and it is plants with thin, delicate leaves which are most at risk. It is important to make sure they are given some shade.

Books and information labels will generally classify your plants as needing full sun, summer shade or all-year shade. The first sort will be best in a south-, south-west- or south-east-facing conservatory if they are to grow and flower well. Plants requiring summer shade will still want good light in winter but prefer the light to be filtered by trees, climbers inside the conservatory or blinds in the summer. (Another solution is to put small plants underneath the tall sun-lovers for the summer.) For a north-facing conservatory, shade plants are ideal and can provide a very effective display as many have evolved large and interesting leaves to catch as much light as possible.

TEMPERATURE

Unfortunately, as the light comes through the glass and gives the plants the energy they need to grow it will also quickly raise the temperature. With no shade and inadequate ventilation, temperatures up to 35°C (95°F) can be reached very quickly. This is uncomfortable for both plants and people, although plants can tolerate high temperatures if you provide good ventilation and they have enough water. It will not normally be the direct effect of the temperature which will cause damage, but the water loss due to the hot, dry air. To allow the carbon dioxide needed for photosynthesis into the plant, the small pores in the leaf, called stomata, must be open and so water will be lost into the air. Keeping the atmosphere humid will help, but eventually the plant will have to shut its stomata, and then growth will come to a stop. The slowing down of growth is bad enough if it goes on for some time, but further loss of water may take place through the leaf surface, especially if the leaves are thin, and you may find that the plant will wilt irreversibly. Never despair, though. This is rare, and normally when you come home to find a plant drooping and looking very sad you will be amazed at how quickly it will recover after it is watered.

underwatering in summer, but certainly appreciate good light. On the other hand plants from the wet tropics will be accustomed to receiving plenty of water and living in temperatures that are high enough for year-round growth. If they grow on the ground in the rainforest they will not want too much light – unless they are climbers. Climbers will need to be given support to reach up to good light.

If you know their origin, common sense will give you a very good idea of how to look after different plants and which ones to choose for the conditions in your conservatory. If you are getting it wrong, spending a few moments just looking around your plants should alert you to any failures in satisfying their needs.

If it is going to be difficult to avoid high temperatures, succulent plants – which have a thick, waxy layer on the leaf – are a good choice because they cope well with water shortage. All plants have a minimum, optimum and maximum temperature for growth and, during the time of year when they are actively growing, a temperature as close as possible to the optimum is preferred. However, this does not mean they cannot survive much lower temperatures than this when they are in a **dormant** state, so give them just enough water to keep them alive in winter as it makes them less vulnerable to lower temperatures.

All plants do have, though, a minimum winter temperature below which they will become damaged and probably die. This means that you have to know what is the minimum temperature that your heating system will maintain in winter when choosing plants. As long as the temperature does not fall below this minimum, a lower temperature for part of the year is helpful as many plants require a resting period. Many climbers, for example, will not flower the next year without this. Plants with bulbs and corms make sure of a rest by dying down and leaving only the resting storage organ. Other plants may indicate their need for a rest by dropping their leaves; when this happens they only need enough water to keep the compost just moist.

If you have a problem with plants, particularly some climbers which in the summer are producing leaves but no flowers, one of the causes can be a lack of a few weeks' rest so it is worth checking if this is a requirement. In most natural environments there are a few weeks when growth slows down or stops. A maximum-minimum thermometer is a very good investment as it enables you to monitor the shifts in temperature and take appropriate action if necessary.

WATER

In an ideal world all watering should be done with rain water and, if there is a water butt collecting the drainage water from the roof of the conservatory, it will be possible to use this for the more sensitive plants such as citrus and orchids. Do remember to allow it to stand inside for a few hours in winter as your plants would not appreciate a sudden deluge of icy water. Equally, tap water should stand for some hours before you use it to lose some of the chlorine and to reach the same temperature as the atmosphere. All this is, of course, a counsel of perfection and when time is short your plants will survive if you rush around with water straight from the tap.

It is important to avoid 'little and often' with watering as all that happens is that the roots come up to the surface instead of spreading through the pot. Enough water should be given each time to a growing plant so it reaches to the bottom

Fig. 6.3 Bananas, such as *Ensete ventricosum*, need large amounts of water during the summer.

of the pot and all the roots. If you are uncertain about how much to give, you can check by removing a young plant from its pot to see if the amount you have given is enough to wet all the compost. You may be surprised to find that the bottom half is quite dry, even when you thought you had watered it well. Another strategy is to water the plant until some drains into the saucer, but this means coming back to empty the saucer when all the water has drained, as standing in water will damage the roots. Some plants, particularly those with hairy leaves, are better watered from below by filling the saucer, because their leaves are damaged by water. They should be left for half an hour to absorb the water and then any still in the saucer can be removed.

How long to wait before watering again depends on the plant. If it comes from a dry area wait until half of the compost is dry; from a temperate area water again when the top 3–4cm (1–1½in) is dry; and with plants from wet areas water as soon as the surface is dry. You can always check this by inserting your finger into the compost. A quick way to check is simply to pick up the pot: if it feels light it means that the compost is dry. If this all sounds impossibly difficult,

Fig. 6.4 *Cordyline fructicosa* 'Kiwi' has green leaves with yellow and red stripes.

don't forget that it is possible to buy various meters which will tell you if water is required.

In the summer some plants may need water every day. This should be done in the evening when the sun is no longer on the plants, otherwise the water will evaporate straight away. It can also do harm to the leaves. Adding **water storage granules** to the compost will help to retain water and allow you to water less often. In winter, when most plants have stopped growing, they will probably only need water once a week or less. Do this in the morning, so that it is absorbed before the temperature falls in the evening.

Every so often a plant, through neglect, will be found with the compost completely dried out. Water will just drain straight through because the spaces between the particles are full of air. When this happens, the pot should be placed in a bucket of water for an hour to allow it to absorb water slowly. If, on the other hand, a plant has been overwatered by an over-zealous helper the best thing to do, if it is possible, is to remove it from its pot to allow the compost to dry out.

Watering of plants in beds is much less time consuming as the compost or soil will not dry out so quickly. However,

because there will probably be a mixture of plants with slightly different requirements, a good general rule is to leave the surface to dry out to a depth of about 3cm (1¼in) and then water thoroughly. Of course, if you have installed an automatic system it is all done for you.

We all tend to water too much or not enough, so once you recognize your own tendency you can adjust your programme accordingly. Remember, however, that more plants have died from overwatering than from underwatering. The symptoms are remarkably similar – pale, wilting leaves and drooping flowers. It is tempting, if a plant looks slightly sad, to give it water but you may be making things worse. If in doubt, don't.

HUMIDITY

Most conservatory plants prefer a slightly humid atmosphere and in the summer, when the air is likely to be dry, will benefit from misting – that is, covering the leaves with a fine spray of water. This is best done in the morning or evening as wet leaves can be damaged by sunlight. Any plant which prefers a more humid atmosphere, such as ferns, can stand

Fig. 6.5 Given time
Blechnum gibbum will
develop a short trunk-
like stem.

on a tray or saucer of damp pebbles, as long as the pot is not standing in liquid water. A group of plants growing together will create its own, more humid microclimate. A more extreme measure altogether is to damp down the entire floor of the conservatory.

In the garden room with a carpeted floor and upholstered furniture none of this is going to be very practical, so one answer is to look through the list of plants and choose those tolerant of a dry environment. Plants from the Mediterranean are a good choice as they are adapted to a hot, dry summer.

FEEDING

Never feed plants unless they are growing because the minerals will just accumulate in the compost, which will then turn sour. This means, for the majority of plants, starting in early spring as soon as growth starts and finishing in autumn.

If you have repotted any plant in fresh compost there will be enough minerals in a soil-based compost for three months and in a peat-based compost enough for six weeks, but after that growing plants will need fertilizer. If in doubt, do not feed. The rule is the same as with watering – too little is less harmful than too much. Too little will slow growth and some old leaves may fall off, but if you overfeed the roots may rot and the leaves wilt. One solution is to add **slow-release fertilizer** in the form of granules which can be mixed into the compost, or tablets or spikes which are pushed into the side of the pot at the beginning of the growing season. They release nutrients at each watering: as the temperature rises and the plants grow faster, more food is released. Cost is a disadvantage, and in a conservatory with more than a few pots a soluble fertilizer used once a week is more economical.

Books recommend a whole range of intervals for feeding, from weekly to monthly, for different plants but remembering

all of this is unrealistic for most of us. A reasonably fail-safe strategy is to add fertilizer to the water on one day each week, perhaps at the weekend when time is less pressing. It may mean that some plants get a little too much, but this is unlikely to cause real harm to plants which are growing. Plants in beds can be fed less often as the fertilizer will not be leached out so readily.

To stimulate leaf growth the best thing is a general fertilizer with equal amounts of nitrogen, phosphorus and potassium, plus very small amounts of trace elements. Once a plant reaches flowering size, however, a fertilizer which contains high amounts of potassium, such as a tomato fertilizer, will encourage flower production. If a plant looks as if it needs a quick stimulus, spraying half strength fertilizer on the leaves (foliar feeding) gives quick results. Epiphytes – plants which in nature grow on trees not in soil, such as some orchids and many bromeliads – will always need to absorb minerals through their leaves.

Although they will grow quite well with the normal fertilizer, there is no doubt that citrus, orchids and acid-loving plants, such as rhododendrons, will do better with their own special product. If you want your lemon tree to produce a fantastic crop, citrus fertilizer will make all the difference.

There are also organic fertilizers on the market for anyone who prefers not to use chemicals. These are based on seaweed or treated manure.

COMPOST

The choice is between a soil-based compost such as a John Innes formula, a multipurpose peat or a specially formulated peat-free compost.

John Innes composts are made from sterilized soil, chalk and peat, with sand added to help with drainage, and a base fertilizer. They can be of variable quality depending on the soil which has been used. If you want to make sure that you are getting a good product it should come from a manufacturer belonging to the John Innes Manufacturers' Association (in the UK), or from a similar organization in other countries. There are two main advantages with a soil-based compost. They are much heavier and give stability to a large plant and the nutrients in the compost last longer. John Innes seed compost is used for germinating seeds or rooting cuttings, No 1 is suitable for young plants in small pots, No 2 for vigorous plants in medium pots and No 3, which is richest in nutrients, for large, very vigorous plants.

Although many multipurpose composts are still peat based, despite the worry about the environmental damage caused by peat extraction, there are now peat free alternatives, based on wood bark, green waste, coir or biosolids, on the market which give good results. Check the label as some products are specially recommended for a particular plant group, and follow advice on watering to avoid overwatering.

The advantages of peat or peat substitute composts are that they are clean and light in weight. They are easier to handle than soil-based composts, but, because nutrients are less easily retained, fertilizer will have to be added sooner. Multipurpose composts can vary a lot in quality; they are suitable for most plants but soil-based are better for large or very vigorous plants such as palms or rampant climbers. Multipurpose composts are cheapest from DIY stores.

If a plant requires free drainage it will grow better if a handful of **perlite**, grit or horticultural sand is mixed with the compost. Another useful addition is **vermiculite**; it absorbs nutrients, then slowly releases them and also retains moisture near the roots.

You will find several special composts at garden centres; orchids, for example, really do need orchid compost as their roots require air and it is worth considering buying an **ericaceous** one if you plan to grow plants such as heaths and rhododendrons. There is also a plant protection compost on the market which claims to protect against vine weevil and some other pests.

In a carpeted garden room, where you want to avoid mess and water spills and have only a few plants, they can be grown in **Seramis** granules. Seramis stores water and releases it as the plant requires it, there is less need for regular watering, there is no need for drainage holes and any type of container can be used. It is a very good medium for growing cacti and other succulents.

REPOTTING

There are several reasons for repotting a plant. In many cases the plant may have grown so well that the pot is full of roots; to grow healthily the plant will need more compost. Some pots may also show an accumulation of excess fertilizer and areas with hard water may have a build up of limescale. Water the plant well and then remove it from the pot, teasing the compost away from the roots, and, if they are spiralling round, gently free them. This is important because when they start growing again they will continue circling around instead of growing out into fresh compost.

Plants should be checked for pests and any dead roots cut away before repotting in a clean pot. If the roots have completely filled the pot, the plant should be moved into a pot that is one size larger, for example from a 12.5cm (5in) to a 15cm (6in) pot. Never be tempted to put it in a much larger pot to save moving it again, the roots will not grow fast enough to take up the water and the compost will turn sour. For most plants the best time to repot is during the early spring – but in an emergency it can be done at anytime.

If using a clay pot, remember to put a piece of broken pot concave side down over the drainage hole. Then add enough compost so that the root ball will come just below the rim of the pot to make watering easier. Add fresh compost around the edges to give a firm, level surface. Always use the same type of compost to avoid upsetting the plant by changing from loam- to peat-based or vice versa. After repotting water well and allow the plant to recover for a few days in the shade. Remember it will not need feeding for a few months.

Eventually a plant will reach an optimum size, so you do not want to encourage it to get any bigger by moving it into a even larger pot. Repotting a plant that is in a 30cm (12in) or larger pot can be a major operation, so this is the time to 'top dress'. This means carefully removing the top 5–7.5cm (2–3in) of compost and replacing it with a fresh layer. From now on this can be done each year and the plant will continue to thrive but growth will be much slower.

Prickly plants can be a problem. One solution is to place the old pot inside the new one and fill round it, leaving a space just big enough for the root ball to be dropped in when the old pot is removed. Repotting is also a good time to remove weeds from the surface of the compost.

Fig. 6.6 A plant will need to be repotted when its roots completely fill the pot.

POTTING UP LILIUM REGALE BULBS

Fig.6.7 Purchase *Lilium regale* bulbs when they become available in the autumn.

Fig. 6.8 Place broken crocks at the bottom of the pot to improve drainage.

Fig. 6.9 Place some compost in the pot and arrange the bulbs on top of it.

Fig. 6.10 Fill the pot with compost, but do not overfill it. The surface of the compost should be about 2cm (¾in) below the rim of the pot.

PRUNING

All plants which flower in summer or autumn should be looked at in late winter to see if any pruning is required. Cutting them back hard by shortening the main shoot and laterals will encourage growth. At the same time any dead, damaged or diseased shoots can be removed. Plants which flower in the winter or spring are best cut back after they have finished flowering. Foliage plants can be pruned to keep them in shape at any time but it is best to avoid any very cold or very hot weather.

The stages of pruning:
1 Remove all dead or diseased material.
2 Cut away any unwanted main stems at soil level.
3 Cut back remaining main stems by required amount (always cutting above a healthy bud).
4 Similarly cut back lateral branches as required.

Once plants are growing again after pruning or young plants have started to grow, the tips of growing shoots can be pinched out to stop them getting too big. This encourages the side shoots to grow out to give a bushy plant.

Finally, to encourage plants to go on flowering longer, keep removing the dead flowers. There is no reason for a plant to keep on flowering once it has produced some seeds.

PESTS

Pests are an inevitable feature of conservatory gardening. By providing warm, sheltered conditions for your plants you are doing the same for pests. However careful you may be in inspecting plants you buy from nurseries or are given by friends, pests will appear after a few months. They will also come in from the garden to this friendly environment. Although the problem tends to get worse in the summer if the conservatory is kept warm in winter, aphids and white fly can remain active, although they will not multiply so fast, and the others will find a cosy place to hibernate. It is a good idea therefore to clean all the surfaces in spring, paying particular attention to any crevices where pests may be lurking. Good hygiene is necessary throughout the year, and it is particularly important to remove any dead plant material, which may harbour potentially damaging pests.

Despite your precautions some pest will manage to invade. The first step is to identify it. The table overleaf lists the most common ones and describes the symptoms. The photographs may also help in identification. Once you know what is attacking your plant you have a choice between using a chemical pesticide or 'integrated pest control'.

There are many proprietary chemical pesticides and the label on what you buy will give a list of which pests they kill. Many of them are **systemic**, which means that once sprayed on they will move upwards inside the plant, so wherever the pest sucks or eats they will be killed, apart from the roots. There are two problems with this. Pests are becoming resistant to many of these products and they are unpleasant. The conservatory is going to be used by people for sitting and eating. Do you really want to use chemical sprays, often with an unpleasant smell and possible harmful effects? If you do decide to use these pesticides you must be careful to avoid contamination. Follow the instructions carefully, only using the recommended strength and frequency of application.

DIAGRAM 5 – HOW TO PRUNE A SHRUB

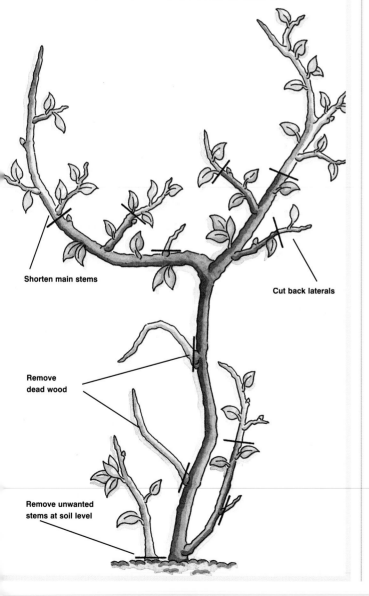

Shorten main stems

Cut back laterals

Remove dead wood

Remove unwanted stems at soil level

Shut any doors into the house and ventilate the conservatory well after spraying. Avoid skin and eye contact. Never spray a stressed plant and do not spray during the hottest part of the day or you may get leaf scorching.

It is these considerations which cause many people to switch to 'integrated pest control'. This approach, now used in the glasshouses of most botanic gardens, uses a combination of safe sprays, natural **predators** and **parasites** to attack the pests. If this strategy is to be used, the first step must be good cultural control so that you see what is happening before there is too much damage or the pest becomes so numerous that it is difficult to control.

Tips of plants and the under-surfaces of leaves are the places to look. If you use a magnifying glass or, if you wear them, reading glasses, it is amazing how many more pests become visible. Look out for stickiness on the leaves, which is a clear sign of pests. Many of them secrete honey dew, so somewhere above the sticky leaf there will be a problem.

Fig. 6.11 One of the best ways to control aphids is to leave the plants outside during the summer. They are quickly eaten by ladybird larvae.

Fig. 6.12 Caterpillars may form their cocoons in rolled-up leaves.

Fig. 6.13 Mealy bugs can be a serious problem with indoor plants.

Fig. 6.14 Root mealy bugs may not be obvious but they can do a lot of damage.

Fig. 6.15 Red spider mite can be controlled by spraying regularly with water.

Fig. 6.16 Scale insects can severely debilitate plants. Use Malathion at full strength.

Fig. 6.17 Severe thrip damage on a rhododendron plant.

Fig. 6.18 Vine weevil is difficult to control, keep your eyes open for the tell-tale notches on leaves. The worst damage is done by the larvae, which eat the succulent roots of plants.

Fig. 6.19 If the infestation is not too severe, white fly can be effectively controlled by using a solution of soft soap.

PEST	SYMPTOMS	SAFE TREATMENT	INSECTICIDE	BIOLOGICAL CONTROL
APHIDS	Green, yellow, pink, grey, brown or black insects under leaves or on tips. Honey dew.	Spray of insecticidal soap or Pyrethrin, Derris.	Pirimicarb (does not harm beneficial insects). Pirimophos-methyl, Permethrin, Bifenthrin.	Aphidius (wasp). Min 10°C (50°F). Aphidoletes (midge). Min 18°C (64°F), long days.
CATERPILLARS	Leaves rolled up or stuck together. Caterpillar inside. Leaves eaten.	Squash the caterpillar. Derris.		*Bacillus thuringiensis.* Do not apply in sun.
MEALY BUG	Wooly patches concealing eggs on stems and leaves. Pale woodlouse-like adults. Honey dew.	Insecticidal soap.	Malathion.	Cryptolaemus (ladybird). Min 18°C (64°F), some sun. Leptomastix (wasps specific to species of mealy bug). Min 25°C (77°F).
ROOT MEALY BUG	White patches on inside of pot and in compost. Stunted plant.	Wash pot and remove infected compost.	Malathion, but not very effective.	None at present.
RED SPIDER MITE	Fine yellow speckling on leaves. Later webbing on leaves and stem. Tiny olive-green insects under leaves. Can be seen with a magnifying glass.	Keep atmosphere humid. Insecticidal soap.	Malathion, Bifenthrin Pirimophos-methyl.	Phytoseiulus (mite). Min 10-18°C (50-64°F). 20°C (68°F) part of the day and good humidity.
SCALE INSECT	Small hard brown or softer pale bumps on stems or leaves. Honey dew.	Remove with thumbnail or with a cotton wool bud dipped in methylated spirits.	Malathion, but very resistant.	Metaphycus (wasp). 22°C (72°F) for some of the day. Good light.
SCIARID FLIES (FUNGUS GNATS)	Flies jumping on surface of compost. White maggots with black heads attacking roots.		Malathion, Permethrin.	Steinernema (nematode). Hypoaspis (mite) in soil. Min 12°C (54°F).
THRIPS	Flecking and silvery trails on leaves, buds and flowers.	Remove affected parts and burn. Pyrethrin.	Permethrin, Malathion, Bifenthrin.	Amblyseius (mite). Min 18°C (64vF). Likes humidity.
VINE WEEVIL	Half-moon shaped notches in leaves. White grubs with brown heads in soil. Black beetles on compost at night.	Use plant protection compost.	Imidacloprid (also effective against aphids, white fly and sciarid fly).	Steinernema (nematode). Heterorhabditis (nematode). Soil temp above 14-21°C (57-70°F).
WHITE FLY	Small white flies when plant disturbed. Resting flies and translucent scales under leaves. Honey dew.	Hand vacuum cleaner. Fatty acid or pyrethrin spray.	Permethrin, Bifethrin.	Encarsia (wasp). Min night temperature 10°C – best 18°C day. Delphastus (ladybird). Min 15°C – best 21°C day.

An unsightly black mould will very quickly start to grow on the honey dew – so this is another indication of trouble.

If an infestation is found, it may be possible to control it by the use of a 'safe spray'. These contain either soft soap or the natural product, pyrethrins. They act as 'contact' insecticides, which means only insects touched by the spray will be killed, so there will be little danger to any harmless insects. However, it does mean that you have to take care when spraying to reach pests under the leaves and in crevices where they may be lurking.

The long-term strategy, however, is to introduce a natural enemy of the pest. As the systemic pesticides and fungicides will act against these enemies as well as against the pests, it is essential to wait three months after spraying with a systemic pesticide before introducing them and to make sure any plants you buy have not already been sprayed. In the meantime, numbers should be controlled with safe sprays as the predators often cannot cope with very heavy infestations, although with a pyrethrin spray you should stop using it four days before introducing the predator. For a small plant, an easy way of controlling pests is to dunk the whole plant in warm, soapy water.

As soon as possible try to identify the pest from the above photographs and see what is the appropriate immediate treatment and the name of its natural enemy. When conditions are suitable you should introduce the natural enemy quickly before the infestation is too heavy for them to control. Most predators and parasites need a daytime temperature of at least 15°C (59°F) and bright daylight for part of the day – so they have to be reintroduced each year. It is obviously pointless to introduce them until the particular pest on which they prey is present or they will starve. Equally they cannot wipe out a pest completely as they are dependant on it for food; the aim is to achieve a natural balance which will give your plants a fair chance. After all, a few small white flies are not going to harm an otherwise healthy plant.

This may all sound complicated but once you have identified what is attacking your plants you can either send away to a specialist supplier for the appropriate predator or parasite (which will arrive with instructions on how to release them) or seek the help of a local garden centre. A cheaper and easier strategy, which is often effective, is to put the plant outside for a few weeks.

DISEASES

There are some fungal diseases which may attack your plants but if you provide good growing conditions they should not normally be a problem.

Grey mould – one of the two you are most likely to come across – looks exactly as the name suggests. A grey fur

Fig. 6.20 Mildew can be a serious problem. Use a systemic fungicide to treat it unless you have integrated pest control.

appears on affected parts, usually on the leaves. These may later fall off if it is a severe attack. It is encouraged by cool temperatures, poor light and a humid, badly ventilated atmosphere. It is more likely to develop if plants are crowded together so that air movement is restricted. So if it occurs, correct the conditions and cut away affected parts. A safe treatment is to dust with sulphur. If you want to use a fungicide, carbendazin is effective but cannot be used if you have introduced biological control insects.

Powdery mildew can grow on leaves, stems and flowers and produces white, powdery patches. A severe attack will weaken the plant. The conditions which favour the growth of the fungus are high temperatures, dry compost and, again, local, damp air due to overcrowding. Again removing the affected parts and dusting with sulphur will protect a plant. As long as you are providing the right conditions you should not find these two diseases a problem. If you do get a bad attack, perhaps because you have been away, you can use a systemic fungicide to control it. You have to remember they cannot be used if you have introduced a predator or parasite to control a pest. The best remedy then is to remove all the affected parts and isolate the plant. In summer time, putting the plants outside can help to get rid of the infection.

The sooty mould which grows on leaves with honey dew has already been mentioned. It is not harmful but is unsightly and may clog up the leaves. A damp cloth can be used to sponge it off.

Fig. 6.21 Citrus plants are prone to infestation by scale insects. They exude 'honey dew', which is then colonised by sooty moulds.

Fig. 6.22 Badly stored bulbs can become infected by grey moulds. Flowers of sulphur is a good way of controlling it.

VIRUS DISEASES

The symptoms are many and varied. The leaves often curl up and may become mottled and distorted, as can buds and flowers. There is no cure, either destroy the plant, or put it outside in an isolated position and monitor its growth. Recovery does sometimes take place. Most viruses are transmitted to another plant when they are pruned or dead-headed with infected secateurs. If this happens it is a good idea to sterilize your secateurs.

REJUVENATION

Every now and then, because of pests, weather, absence or neglect, plants will look sad and unhealthy. If this happens in summer, for any but the most tender plants, the best treatment is a few weeks outside in a sheltered spot. Plants can also become so infested with pests that this is the best way of controlling them.

If this does not effect a cure and if the plant is looking straggly and unattractive, try cutting it back to within a few inches of the compost. This is best done in the spring but in an emergency it is always worth trying at any time of year. Once cut back, the plant should be left in a good light, but away from direct sunlight. If the pot is overcrowded with a lot of rather sorry-looking, mature leaves the plant can be taken out and the younger section from the edge cut off and replanted, with the remainder being discarded.

HOLIDAY CARE

One answer is to only go away in the winter, when a weekly visit by someone to check the plants is all that is required. Unfortunately this is not likely to be a practical solution. If you are going away in summer, move all except the most tender plants outside to a sheltered spot where they will be in the shade for part of the day. They will need very little care unless there is a long, hot, dry spell. If there are gaps in a flower border the pots can be sunk in the soil. This will mean less water loss from the pot and will provide welcome colour to the border on your return.

Tender plants will have to remain inside but they can be grouped together on the floor or a shelf, preferably away from direct sunlight, on a piece of capillary matting, one end of which is in a reservoir of water. Plants in plastic pots, where the compost is in close contact with the matting, will be able to absorb water. The others will benefit from the humid microclimate and will need much less watering. Make sure the plants are healthy before you leave as this type of microclimate is also ideal for pests.

Large climbers are a problem as it is not usually possible to move them, but the pots can be placed on a tray of damp gravel – which will help. If there is no one available to check the plants, one possible solution is that in many areas people offer a service feeding cats when their owners are away and they are often happy to look after plants for the same fee.

DIAGRAM 8 – A PLANTING PLAN TO SHOW PLANTS AT THEIR BEST

This design allows plants to be enjoyed at their best

TO GARDEN

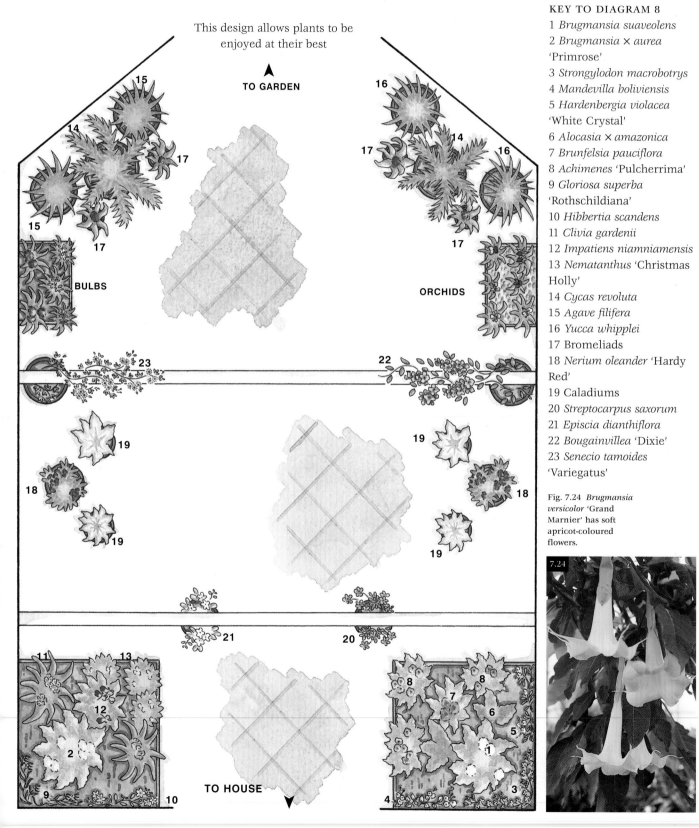

BULBS

ORCHIDS

TO HOUSE

KEY TO DIAGRAM 8

1 *Brugmansia suaveolens*
2 *Brugmansia × aurea* 'Primrose'
3 *Strongylodon macrobotrys*
4 *Mandevilla boliviensis*
5 *Hardenbergia violacea* 'White Crystal'
6 *Alocasia × amazonica*
7 *Brunfelsia pauciflora*
8 *Achimenes* 'Pulcherrima'
9 *Gloriosa superba* 'Rothschildiana'
10 *Hibbertia scandens*
11 *Clivia gardenii*
12 *Impatiens niamniamensis*
13 *Nematanthus* 'Christmas Holly'
14 *Cycas revoluta*
15 *Agave filifera*
16 *Yucca whipplei*
17 Bromeliads
18 *Nerium oleander* 'Hardy Red'
19 Caladiums
20 *Streptocarpus saxorum*
21 *Episcia dianthiflora*
22 *Bougainvillea* 'Dixie'
23 *Senecio tamoides* 'Variegatus'

Fig. 7.24 *Brugmansia versicolor* 'Grand Marnier' has soft apricot-coloured flowers.

A CONSERVATORY FOR PLANTS

This is a plan for a south-west-facing building devoted to growing many different exotic plants. It is kept warm and humid. The aim is for variety in form and colour using as many different plants as possible, among them some unusual and more difficult plants. There will probably be some chairs to sit on and enjoy the plants, but they will be fitted in after all the planting.

There are two beds against the house wall which give the chance of growing some large plants. In both, brugmansia, commonly called angels' trumpets, is the main structural plant and they will be encouraged to grow into small trees. In the right-hand bed there is *Brugmansia suaveolens* (1) with white, fragrant trumpets and in the other bed *Brugmansia × aurea* 'Primrose' (2) with fragrant, primrose-yellow flowers. Both have long flowering seasons.

Behind the *Brugmansia suaveolens,* planted in the corner, is the unusual climber *Strongylodon macrobotrys* (3), the jade vine, with its luminous, jade-green flowers. Beside it, *Mandevilla boliviensis* (4), with white flowers and glossy leaves provides a foil. On the other wall, *Hardenbergia violacea* 'White Crystal' (5), has white flowers in late winter and early spring, before the other climbers are in full growth. Under the brugmansia there are two *Alocasia × amazonica* (6), with their large shield-shaped, dark green leaves with contrasting white veins. In the front, the rounded *Brunfelsia pauciflora* (7) and *Achimenes* 'Pulcherrima' (8) with violet flowers, which in the case of the brunfelsia fade to white, complete the colour scheme.

The colours in the left-hand bed are red and yellow. Behind the yellow brugmansia there is the exotic *Gloriosa superba* 'Rothschildiana' (9), a climber with red and yellow flowers. The other climber is *Hibbertia scandens* (10), which has yellow flowers in summer and attractive large, glossy, slightly fleshy leaves. The permanent planting in this bed is completed with two *Clivia gardenii* (11), with whorls of narrow leaves and large, round heads of yellow flowers, plus a cockatoo plant, *Impatiens niamniamensis* (12), with its unusual red and yellow flowers and several low-growing *Nematanthus* 'Christmas Holly' (13) in the front.

The planting by the door into the garden is very different. There is a Sago palm, *Cycas revoluta* (14), at each side. Beside one there are two *Agave filifera* (15), which have narrow leaves – edged with whitish threads. Beside the other palm are two specimens of *Yucca whipplei* (16) with whorls of narrow, spine-tipped leaves. All the plants are linked by their whorls of leaves in different shades of green. In front of each group there are some bromeliads (17) with their colourful flowers and leaves.

Breaking up the long axis and separating the more austere planting from the beds full of flowers there is an oleander, *Nerium oleander* 'Hardy Red' (18) on each side; their dark green leaves echoing those of the cycad. With the oleanders are a selection of caladiums (19), the red markings of the foliage echoing the colour of the oleander flowers.

There is a planter on one side which will be filled with spring bulbs early in the year and later with tender, summer-flowering bulbs. In another planter, pots of orchids are plunged in damp gravel.

On one of the beams there are pots with hanging plants. One pot has *Streptocarpus saxorum* (20) with lilac flowers and soft, hairy, green leaves, while the other is the white-flowered *Episcia dianthiflora* (21). On the other beam, a red-flowered *Bougainvillea* 'Dixie' (22) and *Senecio tamoides* 'Variegatus' (23) complete the display.

Fig. 7.21 *Senecio tamoides* has attractive bright yellow flowers.

Fig. 7.22 The flowers of *Impatiens niamniamensis* look like a line of cockatoos.

Fig. 7.23 *Mandevilla splendens* is a very pretty exotic climber.

the year, is growing in front of a glossy-leaved *Ficus lyrata* and adds some bright colour to the display. In the shade under the tetrastigma, there are two plants of begonia 'Burle Marx' (10). This has crinkled leaves, with a hint of red, and tall, white flowers in summer.

Finally, a possible position for some seasonal planting of bulbs or decorative plants (11) is indicated on the plan.

PLAN FOR PEOPLE AND PLANTS

This conservatory is a high, lean-to design, which faces towards the south. The house wall forms the back of the structure. It is used for sitting and informal meals. Colour and fragrance throughout the year were the aims, with an emphasis on pink, mauve and blue colours.

In this plan, even before considering the structural plants, the priority was to decide which species to use to cover the large expanse of wall at the back. Four vigorous climbers, which like good light and have long flowering seasons, were chosen: pink bougainvillea 'Donyo' (1), which should be in flower for much of the year; blue *Plumbago auriculata* (2), flowering in summer and autumn; violet *Hardenbergia violacea* (3), giving winter and spring flowers; and pale pink *Ipomoea carnea* (4), which is in flower from spring to autumn. Beneath these there are two structural plants which will shield the bare stems at the base of the climbers – these are

the Abyssinian banana, *Ensete ventricosum* (5), with its huge leaves which can measure up to 150cm (5ft) long, and *Sparrmannia africana* (6), which also has large leaves and bunches of white flowers in winter.

In front of the banana, colour comes from the lilac flowers of the rounded *Cuphea hyssopifolia* (7). *Anisodontea capensis* (8) is a similar shape but has tiny, pink flowers from spring to winter. In the other corner is the almost continuously flowering *Alyogyne huegelii* 'Santa Cruz' (9), which has beautiful blue flowers. This is flanked by two winter-flowering *Luculia gratissima* 'Early Dawn' (10), with deep pink, very fragrant flowers.

In the bed opposite the door from the house there is a *Justicia carnea* (11) with large, ribbed leaves and big, round groups of pink flowers in summer. The front of the bed will be used for seasonal planting (12) and the evergreen foliage background on each side of the *Justicia carnea* is provided by two low-growing *Pittosporum tobira* 'Nanum' (13) with small, scented flowers. Another species of justicia, *J. rizzinii*, has scarlet flowers with yellow tips.

Finally, on either side of the door into the garden, there are two plants of *Citrus × meyeri* 'Meyer' (14). This is a very vigorous hybrid lemon, which flowers throughout the year. It is easy to grow and readily available from garden centres. The yellow lemons do not fit in perfectly with the overall colour scheme, but rules are made to be broken and they will add wonderful scent and provide fruit to pick.

Fig. 7.19 *Sparrmannia africana* will grow to a height of over 90cm (3ft) in a conservatory.

Fig. 7.20 Citrus blossom produces a sweet fragrance, which can be almost overpowering in an enclosed room.

DIAGRAM 7 – A PLANTING PLAN SUITABLE FOR PEOPLE AND PLANTS

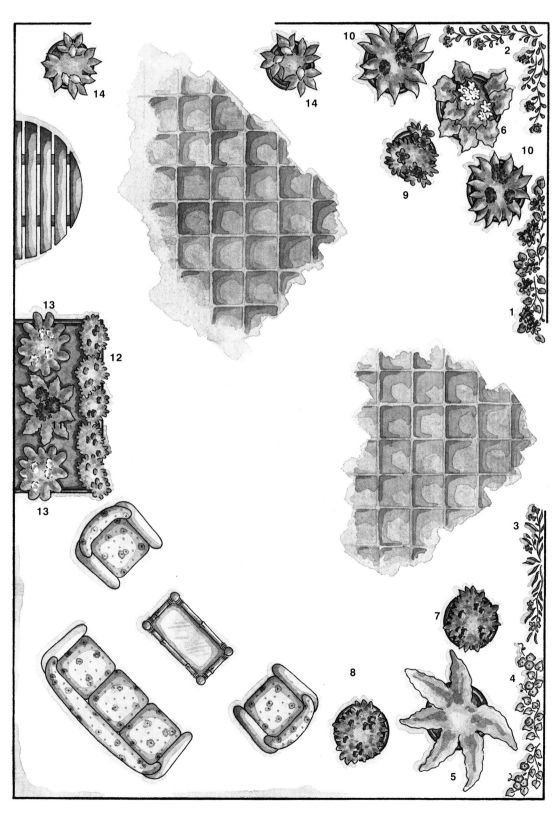

This conservatory design is comfortable to sit in, yet it allows plants to thrive.

KEY TO DIAGRAM 7
1 *Bougainvillea* 'Donyo'
2 *Plumbago auriculata*
3 *Hardenbergia violacea*
4 *Ipomoea carnea*
5 *Ensete ventricosum*
6 *Sparrmannia africana*
7 *Cuphea hyssopifolia*
8 *Anisodontea capensis*
9 *Alyogyne huegelii* 'Santa Cruz'
10 *Luculia gratissima* 'Early Dawn'
11 *Justicia carnea*
12 Seasonal planting
13 *Pittosporum tobira* 'Nanum'
14 *Citrus x meyeri* 'Meyer'

Fig. 7.10 Oriental lilies have large flamboyant flowers. The bulbs are readily available from garden centres. This hybrid cultivar is called 'Satre'.

Fig. 7.11 Laeliocattleyas need a minimum night temperature of 13°C (55°F), but they have gorgeous flowers.

BULBS

If you choose them carefully it is possible to have tender bulbs in flower at all times of year, many with exotic, unusual blooms and long flowering periods. They can be used to add colour and interest to a group. After they have flowered, most of them should be allowed to dry and then stored in a cool place until it is time to replant.

A cool conservatory with a minimum night temperature of 7–10°C (45–50°C) is suitable for all except a few tropical species. Many of them like as much light as possible, particularly the winter-flowering species, but there are also bulbs, such as calla lilies, for a shady position.

In addition to the tender bulbs, you can start spring early by planting some of the spring-flowering garden bulbs in the conservatory, and this will give you a display of narcissi and daffodils while it is still winter outside. Once they have finished flowering they can be planted outside to grace your garden the following year.

ORCHIDS

The orchids belong to one of the largest plant families and in addition there are many thousands of artificially created hybrids. The flowers are incredibly varied in colour, shape and size – some are quite extraordinary.

Although they have a reputation for being difficult to grow, it is worth considering trying to grow one of the easier **hybrids**, such as a cymbidium. As long as you give it humid conditions and use a special fertilizer, they should reward you with spectacular flowers. They can be grown in pots, preferably in a special orchid compost, or the epiphytic species can be attached to a tree trunk, possibly mixed with some bromeliads. The result will be a display which all your visitors will admire. If you are successful you may find that you'll become one of the growing number of people who find orchid growing an absorbing hobby. Flower shows are a good place to see a range of orchids.

CITRUS FRUIT

If you want fragrant blossom, attractive, glossy foliage and the chance to pick your own lemons or oranges, then try to find space for a citrus plant in your conservatory. All they need is a cool conservatory, a special fertilizer and, if it is possible, a few weeks outside in summer. You will be amply rewarded for your trouble. You may find they look best grown as specimen plants rather than with other species in a group. They look particularly effective with a pair used on either side of a door – as long as draughts can be avoided.

SAFETY

Some plants are harmful if they are eaten, others may cause a skin reaction if they are handled, while some have sharp points to their leaves or nasty thorns. While none of these characteristics need mean not growing these plants, it is as well to be aware of possible dangers when choosing which species to grow. In the lists of plants later in the book, any which are known to be potentially harmful are identified, but remember that the fact that a plant is not identified as poisonous does not mean that it is safe to eat.

PLANTING PLANS

After reading about all the plants which you could grow and possibly seeing some of them in nurseries or botanic gardens, it is time to be practical and make a rough scale plan, including the position of any furniture, to see how your ideas can be fitted into the space available. You can decide where you want plants and work out how many there will be room for. In some spots there will only be space for a single specimen plant, in others there will be room for a group of plants on the floor, a window sill or displayed on a **jardiniere**. You can also identify where climbers can grow and whether it would be possible to have a hanging basket or two.

The best way to start is to decide where the structural plants and climbers will go in the conservatory and then add the shrubs and perennials which will complement them. After this comes the difficult stage of choosing which plants to use. The best plants are those which will be adapted to the conditions and give a harmonious display. There is obviously little point is trying to grow plants that like shady, humid, conditions in a bright sunny conservatory without any shading. Some plants may look very attractive in the garden centre but prove difficult to grow in a conservatory.

To help you choose the best plants for your conservatory I have included three sample plans. The recommended plants which feature in them will be discussed in more detail in the forthcoming chapters.

Fig. 7.12 Citrus trees look good in terracotta pots or Versailles containers.

A SHADED GARDEN ROOM

This room (diagram 6) is used as a sitting room and for informal dining. Plants are needed to give a restful background to brightly coloured furniture and the leaded windows, and the emphasis is on evergreen foliage plants with strong shapes. The colours are restricted – mainly white with hints of red in some of the foliage, and the red flowers of the anthuriums.

Structural plants in each corner help soften the rectangular shape. All of those in the plan are linked by their arching leaves. There is *Phoenix roebelenii*, the pygmy date palm (1), in the corner behind the sofa and *Ficus lyrata*, the large-leaved fiddle-leaf fig (2), by the archway to the kitchen. In the other two corners are *Cordyline australis* 'Red Star' (3), with bronzy red foliage planted behind the dining table and *Strelitzia reginae*, the bird of paradise (4). For a simpler effect the same plant could be planted in two or more corners or two varieties of the same plant, for example, several different cordylines could be used. To draw attention to the door in to

DIAGRAM 6 – A SUGGESTED PLANTING PLAN FOR A GARDEN ROOM

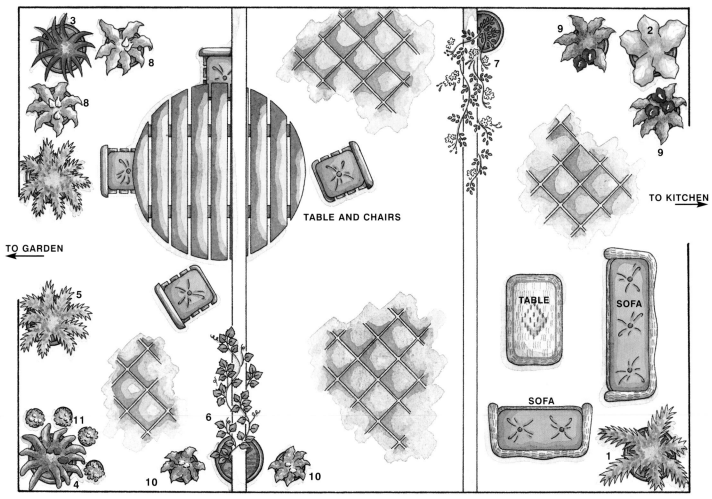

TO KITCHEN

TABLE AND CHAIRS

TO GARDEN

TABLE

SOFA

SOFA

the garden and the view from it there are two *Blechnum gibbum*, the dwarf tree fern (5).

The beams provide an ideal support for climbers to soften the impact of a timber and plaster roof. A tough, fast-growing evergreen such as *Tetrastigma voinierianum*, the chestnut vine (6), with its horse chestnut-shaped leaves, is needed to cope with the poor light on the north side of the conservatory. Where the light is better on the other side there is *Jasminum sambac* (7), an evergreen climber which should produce white, fragrant flowers almost continuously in the warm conditions of this garden room. Later on, once the original plants have grown, more climbers could be planted if it was felt they were needed.

Lastly there are the shrubs and perennials to complete the planting. In one corner there are white-flowered peace lilies, *Spathiphyllum wallisii* (8), to complement the *Cordyline indivisa* with its red-tinged leaves. In another corner, *Anthurium scherzerianum* (9), which has bright red 'flowers' throughout

KEY TO DIAGRAM 6
1 *Phoenix roebelenii*
2 *Ficus lyrata*
3 *Cordyline australis* 'Red Star'
4 *Strelitzia reginae*
5 *Blechnum gibbum*
6 *Tetrastigma voinierianum*
7 *Jasminum sambac*
8 *Spathiphyllum wallisii*
9 *Anthurium scherzerianum*
10 *Begonia* 'Burle Marx'
11 Bulbs and decorative plants

See the following pages for some of the plants used in this plan

7.13

7.14

7.18

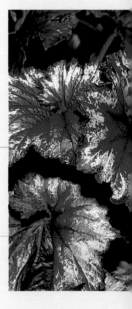

Fig. 7.13 *Justicia rizzinii* is an attractive shrub which flowers from late autumn to early spring.

Fig. 7.14 *Dracaena fragrans* 'Warneckei' has lanceolate bright green leaves with two white stripes.

Fig. 7.15 Lemon trees have wonderful scented flowers and edible fruit.

Fig. 7.16 Arabian jasmine (*Jasminum sambac*) is an evergreen climber with highly fragrant waxy white flowers.

Fig. 7.17 Begonia 'Raspberry Swirl' has shiny raspberry-red foliage.

Fig. 7.18 *Plumbago auriculata* has pretty sky-blue flowers. It is inclined to become a bit straggly and therefore needs to be pruned regularly.

Fig. 7.8 Bromeliad trees are one of the most effective ways of showing these epiphytic plants.

Fig. 7.9 Cacti are very popular green-house plants, but they can also be grown successfully in a conservatory.

of temperatures, as long as they are protected from frost. Most species prefer bright light, which will help to bring out the leaf colours and markings, and a humid atmosphere – but they will tolerate shade and drier air. The majority of them are **epiphytes**, that is they grow on trees and shrubs using their roots only for anchorage and absorbing water and minerals through their leaves. In many common species the leaves form a cup to collect water and debris. It is important to keep this reservoir topped up with water and to mist the leaves of the species without reservoirs. All of them can be grown in pots in free-draining compost but to mimic their natural habitat their roots can be wrapped in sphagnum moss and the plant attached to a log to make an unusual feature.

CACTI AND SUCCULENTS

These are the plants which are adapted to survive under conditions where there is little water for long periods – so they are an obvious choice for those who are going to forget

to water. They are nearly all plants which will survive when neglected. During their growing season they like good light and ideally should be watered at least once a week. This is in contrast with most conservatory plants in summer which may need daily watering. In winter, apart from the few winter-growing species, they require a cool, dry rest. The growing medium should be very porous so adding some sand or grit to the compost is a good idea. Given the correct conditions some species can grow to a substantial size.

Succulents look best when they are grown together, but as they come in a wide diversity of shapes, sizes and colour it is easy to create a spectacular display. For example there are large, spiky agaves to provide a focal point, which can be surrounded by plants forming tall columns or spiky pads. Colour and interest can then be added by planting smaller species, many of which are free-flowering, in the front of the display. Adding some of the winter-flowering crassulas will extend the season of interest.

blues and violets which will make a small space appear larger. Or you may prefer 'hot' reds, oranges and yellows. Using contrasting colours, such as yellow with purple or orange with blue, will achieve a more dramatic display. The colour of the leaves of the foliage plants will make an important contribution and should complement the colour of the flowers: you might choose plants with grey leaves to set off pink and blue flowers; white and green variegated leaves to set off whites or reds; or orange-tinted leaves with orange flowers.

Just as with structural planting, the plants within a group should be linked by at least one characteristic. While it would be boring to have a group all with large, glossy, dark green, arching leaves, it could be brought alight by adding a vertical plant with small, feathery, dark green leaves as a contrast. The overall shape of the group should also be borne in mind. A tall, spiky plant can be highlighted by **underplanting** to give a mound effect, or a tall, arching plant can be offset by a domed-shape plant beneath it.

Using the same or a very similar plant in different groups will help to bring the entire display together. Examples would be placing a pink oleander in one group and one with cream-coloured flowers in another corner, or planting several caladiums with different leaf colourings.

SEASONAL PLANTS

These are the plants that can be brought in to add colour at different times of the year, such as cyclamens in winter and streptocarpus in summer. They are often thought of as short-term plants, but if the winter-flowering ones can be left outside in a sheltered spot in summer and there is an out of the way corner in the conservatory for the summer-flowering ones to spend the winter, there is no reason why they should not survive for many years.

TRAILING PLANTS

These, like climbing plants, add an extra dimension to a display without taking up valuable space. In their natural habitat trailing plants are supported by other vegetation, but in cultivation they have to be tied to supports. There are many flowering hanging plants that will continue to flower from spring to late autumn, several of which are described in the following chapters. Other trailing plants are grown for their foliage. The only problem with these plants is watering them: they can lose water quickly and may be awkward to reach if they are suspended from the ceiling.

Trailing plants at the edge of a planting bed or a sill can add the finishing touch to a group and hide the coping of the bed or cover up a boring expanse of wall. They also look good growing over the wall at the edge of a raised pond.

PALMS

Palms are one of the most popular groups of structural plants for the conservatory. A wide range is available, including some with spectacular fan-shaped leaves and others with feathery, arching fronds. Leaf colours range from dark green to bright green. There are even palms with blue leaves. It is easy to think of palms as desert plants growing in strong light and dry air, but to grow well most of them require some shade and a humid atmosphere. Luckily there are some exceptions, like the date palm, which will tolerate a hot, dry conservatory, but if you are able to maintain a humid atmosphere there is now a bewildering choice of palms. You may get so enthusiastic after a visit to a specialist nursery that you decide to throw out the conservatory carpet and upholstered furniture and choose to give some exotic palms the humidity that they need.

As more and more palms are being found to be hardy, particularly older plants, a conservatory palm that gets too big can be planted out to give your garden a touch of the fashionable exotic look.

FERNS

Few groups of plants recall the Victorian era as much as the ferns. A typical Victorian conservatory was full of beautiful ferns. They helped to create the impression of a lush tropical jungle and were widely collected.

As long as you can provide the shade they need, using blinds or other plants, you can produce this effect in your conservatory. You have the choice of using large, imposing tree ferns as structural plants or growing groups of ferns. A planter can be used for five or six ferns, chosen to show off the variety of foliage, including some like the maidenhair fern with delicate, feathery **fronds**, others with strap-shaped fronds and some with stiff, upright fronds. A group of ferns will also make effective underplanting beneath a tall plant or around a water feature. As a specimen plant, the staghorn fern, with its green, fleshy fronds – which really do look like a stag's horns – looks exotic planted in a wall pot or grown on a moss-covered log. Trailing ferns make good hanging basket plants in a shaded conservatory.

BROMELIADS

The bromeliads produce some of the most unusual and eye-catching flowers in amazing colour combinations. The flowers last for weeks, the foliage is attractive and some have unusual and colourful fruits – so there is every reason to consider adding some bromeliads to a conservatory. They are very easy to grow and tolerate most conditions and a wide range

CLIMBERS

Climbing plants can transform a conservatory. They take up very little space but make an instant impact and provide a vertical element to the planting. The more vigorous growers can be trained over the roof to give necessary shade in summer and may, as suggested before, allow you to dispense with expensive blinds. The less vigorous can be planted to climb through a shrub to give colour when it has finished flowering or to conceal the bare trunk. Their foliage and flowers will give a wonderful display against a wall.

By planting two or more species together you can ensure that the floral display lasts for much of the year. Some climbers are always deciduous, that is, they lose their leaves in winter, but with others it will depend upon the temperature and light levels. Their behaviour can even vary from year to year. It is not a matter of concern if they do lose their leaves: the enforced rest may even spur them on to flower more profusely next summer. Some summer-flowering climbers, such as a morning glory, always lose their leaves and leave you with a bare wall. To avoid this, plant other species as well, such as the winter-flowering hardenbergia or a jasmine for scent and flowers in early spring.

Climbing plants are mostly very vigorous. Planting them in a bed will give them a chance to reach right up to the roof or over it, but as long as they are in a large pot in good compost with plenty of water and fertilizer during their growing period they will soon cover a large area. Many of the flowering climbers require good light as they are adapted to climbing up to the light in the tropical or semitropical forest from where they come. The climbers which will do well in a low light are some of the evergreens with interesting foliage, such as the well-known philodendron or rhoicissus. Even if there is no convenient wall or other support you can still add height to a display by growing climbing plants up a pyramid support in a large pot.

There are over 350 species of philodendron, many of which can be grown in the conservatory. They orginate from Southern America and can be trained to grow around a moss-covered pole. Some species have cultivars with pink, red or variegated leaves.

SHRUBS AND PERENNIALS

These are the plants which highlight the structural plants and add colour and interest by their foliage and flowers. Foliage plants, with their many different colours, shapes and textures, give interest all year round. Others can be chosen chiefly for their flowers. Many have a long flowering season, so that with the right choice of plants it is possible to have flowers throughout the year. The colours can be the cool greens,

7.6

7.7

Fig. 7.6 *Neodypsis decaryi* is a very distinctive looking palm, which originates from Madagascar.

Fig. 7.7 The Chusan palm, *Trachycarpus fortunei*, is frost hardy in a sheltered spot, but if you wish it can be brought into the conservatory during winter.

Fig.7.5 The sago palm (*Cycas revoluta*) will grow happily in a large pot of John Innes No 3 compost. In Mediterranean countries it forms a small, stout tree.

STRUCTURAL PLANTS

One of the first considerations in planting a conservatory should be to use plants with architectural features as focal points, just as they are in a garden. These plants, which are usually evergreens, have a strong shape or texture. They may be exotic-looking, as is the case with the spiky furcraeas, or, like the bananas, make their impact with large, glossy leaves. However they all have a naturally sculptured form, in strong contrast to other plants, which may be rather amorphous and have no distinct shape.

These are the plants which, either used by themselves as a specimen or featuring as the focal point of a group, are going to make the greatest impact. They should therefore be the first to be placed in position. Architectural plants will provide interest all year round and form a background for other more decorative planting.

When you have chosen where you want to place the plants you should select a structural plant to provide the focus for each group. You can use the same or very similar plants to achieve the harmony which comes from simplicity of design or you can be more adventurous.

If you want a display incorporating plants with different shapes or habit, choose one characteristic which links them together. If you have a spiky aloe in one corner and a palm in another, for example, there will be a sharp contrast of shapes. If you choose varieties with blue foliage, however, they could be linked together by their colour, the contrast in form adding vitality to the design. Alternatively a drooping cupressus with its fine foliage would complement a weeping fig because, although they have a different texture, they share a similar shape.

A conservatory can often end up as being nothing more than a comfortable place to sit in, with a few plants scattered around. The opportunity to create something better, with just a few more plants, has been ignored. The plants have not been chosen in order to produce harmony. The sense of unity which could have been created by using plants with a similar origin, habit or shape has not been achieved. All too often, gardeners who would never dream of mixing two styles in a garden will scatter plants around their conservatory with no clear idea of what effect they are hoping to achieve.

Perhaps it is the problem of choice. Plants are available from all over the world to entice the new conservatory owner. They come from deserts, tropical rainforests, mountains and lowlands. Catalogues show plants from every continent. How tempting, therefore, to remember the brilliant colour of bougainvillea in the South of France, the dramatic outline of palms in North Africa or the fragrance of mimosa in the Middle East during the spring – and to want them all. However, it is rare to see a conservatory where all of the plants have been chosen with a clear, linking theme. When one visits a glasshouse where the plants have a common origin – perhaps the drier regions of Australia – the impact is immediate. The plants complement each other and the display achieves a restful harmony. This is so different from the frequent sight of a yucca sitting beside a calathea with some pelargoniums as uneasy companions.

When you are selecting plants for the conservatory it is important to remember the conditions that prevail within it. If there is a shady border with acid soil in your garden, you would normally choose plants which will thrive there. So you should do the same for a south-facing conservatory with limited ventilation. The main factor in determining the most suitable plants will be the minimum temperature that can be maintained during the winter. Disappointment is normally the result of choosing the wrong plants for the temperature, humidity and aspect of the conservatory, or underestimating the time that is required to care for delicate plants. The owner should have aimed for fewer, healthier plants, linked by a common theme.

You may want to choose plants with varying shades of the same colour or experiment with bold contrasts. Pink with orange, or orange with purple, will make a bold statement. Fragrance is yet another quality to be borne in mind when you are planning what you will grow. Smelling the scent of a lemon or heliotrope as you come into a conservatory lifts the spirits and with careful choice you can have scent for much of the year.

Previous page
Fig. 7.1
Gloriosa superba 'Rothschildiana' is an exotic looking climber with vivid scarlet red flowers.

Fig. 7.2
Furcraea longaeva is often mistaken for a yucca, to which it is related. It bears large panicles of cream-coloured flowers.

Fig. 7.3 *Cordyline australis* is a fast growing tree. It will grow happily in a pot and makes a superb architectural plant.

Fig. 7.4 Cordylines can be used as the focal point for a planting. This one is surrounded by the succulent *Aloe arborescens*.

CHAPTER

7

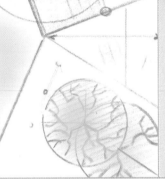

DESIGNING
WITH
PLANTS

CHAPTER  8

PLANTS FOR A
GARDEN ROOM

A garden room is for sitting and dining while you enjoy the garden and sky from indoors. Although space may be limited, you may still want the pleasure of living close to plants. When choosing them for a garden room you want to avoid those which need a lot of care. Plants which are very demanding about their living conditions are not for a garden room and neither are those which need high humidity. It may also be difficult to accommodate plants which require a cool, winter rest period.

The day temperature in a garden room will normally be kept around a comfortable 20°C (68°F), but for the plants the night temperature will also be important. Therefore, check just how cold it gets on a winter night before choosing a plant which needs a minimum of 10°C (50°F). There are some in the lists below which will tolerate warm days and cold nights, while for some of the others a position against a house wall will provide enough protection.

The other factor which will affect choice is the amount of light and how much shade there will be from direct sunlight in summer.

There are many hundreds of conservatory plants which is what makes selection so difficult. This chapter describes some plants which would be suitable for growing in a garden room. Some are well-known favourites because they are reliable and easy to find, others are more unusual. Unless some special requirement is mentioned all you will need to do is follow the general advice on care in Chapter 6, and remember most plants will withstand some neglect.

STRUCTURAL PLANTS

Chamaedorea elegans, the parlour palm, may be well known but this is because it is so tolerant of poor light, dry air, warm days and cold nights. It is more compact than some other palms but can grow to 2–3m (6–9ft). It has a short, green trunk and long, arching leaves divided into leaflets.
A soil-based compost is best and it should be kept moist in the growing season, but allow the top few inches of compost to dry out before watering in winter. If the tips of the leaves turn brown it will be because of dry air so either mist the leaves or stand the pot on a saucer of damp gravel.
Feed occasionally in summer. Like all palms it likes to be pot-bound so it should not be repotted until the roots completely fill the pot.

Chamaerops humilis, the Mediterranean fan palm, is another tough plant but differs in that it requires bright light. The fan-shaped leaves spread out so it does need space. It should be cared for in the same way as the parlour palm. It can be put outside in summer to decorate the patio.

Rhapis excelsa, the lady palm, is also tolerant of dry air but prefers indirect light. It grows more slowly, so it is a good choice if space is restricted. The glossy, fan-shaped leaves grow all the way down to the base. Care is the same and growth can be restricted by leaving it in a 16cm (6½in) pot and top dressing in spring.

Phoenix roebelenii, the pygmy date palm, likes filtered light but can be grown successfully in bright light. With its feather-

Previous page
Fig. 8.1 **The glorybush (*Tibouchina urvilleana*)** has vivid mauve or violet flowers. It needs to be pruned back in the spring to stop it from becoming straggly.

Fig. 8.2 *Chamaerops humilis* **is a native of southern Europe. It is quite hardy and makes a good conservatory plant. It can be placed outside during the summer.**

Fig. 8.3 (left) **The lady palm (*Rhapsis excelsa*) is a superb plant. It tolerates low light levels, but it must not be allowed to dry out.**

Fig. 8.4 (right) *Dracaena frgarans* **'Massangeana' produces rosettes of yellow-striped green leaves. As the plant grows it sheds the older leaves to leave a bare trunk.**

8.4

shaped leaves it is a perfect miniature palm. It is best in a well-drained peat compost so put plenty of crocks at the base of the pot. It likes plenty of water in summer and prefers to be pot-bound so it will be several years before it needs repotting. If the leaves turn yellow it may be due to lack of iron, which can be cured with a dose of **Sesquesterone**.

Dracaena fragrans (corn plant) cultivars are a large and varied group of plants. They like warmth but can withstand cool conditions. Good indirect light is best. They all have stout, upright stems with rosettes of leaves at the top and you can find plants with white, yellow or even pink and cream variegation. After a few years they may become leggy and unattractive but, if you cut off the top, they grow again from the upper part of the stem. Soil-based compost with plenty of drainage material in the base is best. They can be grown successfully in quite small pots for a number of years. Normal watering and feeding during the growing season is all that is required for it to do well.

Citrus ✕ *meyeri* 'Meyer', Meyer's lemon, or ✕ *Citrofortunella microcarpa,* the calamondin orange, can be put outside when it gets too hot in summer. Well-drained, slightly acid compost is best so you could consider using ericaceous compost. A light dusting with flowers of sulphur two or three times a year will ensure that the pH of the compost is correct. They prefer rain water and dislike overwatering, particularly in winter. If you use special citrus fertilizer, which is widely available in garden centres, you will be rewarded by a good crop of fruit. Lemon trees can withstand cool conditions but calamondin oranges need a minimum of 15°C (59°F).

CLIMBERS

Ipomoea indica and *I. carnea,* perennial morning glories, are easy, fast-growing and will be in flower from spring right through to the late autumn, with the added advantage of having attractive heart-shaped leaves. *Ipomoea indica* has intensely blue flowers and *I. carnea* pale mauve flowers. They are best in John Innes No 3 and like good light, plenty of water and weekly fertilizer in summer. A dry resting period in winter will mean more flowers next season. If they get too big they can be cut back after flowering.

Mandevilla ✕ *amoena* 'Alice du Pont' is another easy plant which will produce large, pink flowers over a long period and has glossy, green leaves. The shoots quickly twine around available supports. Care is the same as for ipomoea but it does prefer some shade from direct summer sun and it grows better if it is cut back in the autumn. *Mandevilla sanderi* is a similar plant with rose-pink flowers.

Fig. 8.5 Perennial morning glory (*Ipomoea indica*) is a herbaceous climber with vivid purple or blue flowers.

Fig. 8.7 *Mandevilla* ✕ *aemoena* 'Alice du Pont' is a vigorous climber with bright pink flowers and twining stems.

Fig. 8.6 *Tweedia caerulea* is a small shrub with twining shoots. It originates from South America and has pale blue flowers.

Fig. 8.8 Citrus trees can be pruned into a range of different shapes. They look wonderful in a Versailles container or large terracotta pot.

8. 7

8. 8

Tweedia caerulea is a smaller, more delicate twining plant with hairy, heart-shaped leaves. The flowers, which are produced in spring and summer, are pale blue at first and then change to violet as they mature. The only special care required is that it prefers a soil-based compost and should be cut back to avoid it becoming straggly.

Pandorea jasminoides 'Rosea Superba', bower plant, is another easy, evergreen climber with deep pink flowers in summer and autumn. They are best in good light and can be pruned in spring to keep them from getting too big. There is also a variety with white flowers.

Passiflora × *violacea* is a free-flowering passion flower which does well in a pot. It has violet flowers and likes good light with some protection from summer sun. Weak stems can be cut back in winter. An alternative would be *Passiflora herbertiana* with yellow flowers, which change colour to red or *P. mollissima*, which has pink flowers. They all have a long flowering season.

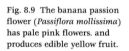

Fig. 8.9 The banana passion flower (*Passiflora mollissima*) has pale pink flowers. and produces edible yellow fruit.

Fig. 8.10 *Leptospermum scoparium* originates from Australia and New Zealand.

Fig. 8.11 *Lantana camara* is an evergreen shrub with clusters of small flowers. There are several different colours available. The variety illustrated is called 'Snow White'.

Fig. 8.16 If you keep repotting it a hibiscus can grow to as much as 1.8m (6ft) in height. There are a wide range of colours available – regular pruning will help to create a nicely shaped bush.

8.16

Tibouchina urvilleana, the glory bush, produces vivid blue flowers from summer right into the early winter and has the added appeal of attractive, velvety leaves. It is very resistant to pests and the only danger is that it can become straggly and may need support. It is important therefore to cut back the main stem by half and shorten the side shoots to two pairs of leaves each spring. It can be put outside in the summer and moved into a larger pot if you want a bigger plant at that time. It prefers a soil-based compost.

Leptospermum scoparium, the south sea myrtle, is a plant for spring flowers. There are several varieties with white, pink or red flowers on a round bush. Once they have finished flowering they can be put outside for the summer and then be brought in again for the winter, ready to start flowering in the early spring. They are tough plants, which need no special care.

Lantana camara, shrub verbena or yellow sage, will come into flower in early summer and be covered with flowers until the autumn. Varieties are available in a wide range of single and mixed colours. Apart from allowing the compost to dry slightly between watering they need no special care. As they are semi-hardy they can be moved outside in the summer. They are poisonous.

Nerium oleander, oleanders, again come in a range of colours: pink, red, yellow, apricot and white. They will be in flower from early summer to late autumn and then should be pruned hard and kept dry for a few weeks to allow them to rest. They like good light, plenty of water, and fertilizer when growing. They can be put outside in summer in a sheltered place and this can be useful if you go on holiday or as a way of getting rid of pests. All oleanders are poisonous.

Heliotropium arborescens, cherry pie, is another plant which will be in flower for most of the year if it is fed regularly. The flowers are very fragrant and there are white, violet and purple varieties. They should be cut back by half in spring to maintain a good shape and repotted in John Innes No 2. They do appreciate misting in summer and the removal of dead flowers and leaves.

Hibiscus rosa-sinensis, rose-of-China, deserves its popularity. Varieties are available in a wide range of colours and, although each flower only lasts one day, with good care you will be rewarded with a continuous display of flowers. Good light is essential with a dry, winter rest and it grows best in a soil-based compost. By careful pruning and pinching out the tips you can encourage it to develop into a standard with a round head on a single stem.

Jatropha integerrima is a graceful plant with clusters of soft, red flowers all summer and right on into the autumn. It is really worth looking for. It likes warmth, good light and normal watering and feeding.

Plumbago auriculata, the Cape leadwort, is possibly the easiest of all shrubs. It produces a profusion of blue or white and flowers from summer until autumn. It should be drastically cut back once flowering has finished as it can be inclined to become rather straggly. There is only one disadvantage – as the flowers die they become sticky and attach themselves to anything that touches them, including your hair and clothes.

FERNS

Nephrolepis cordifolia, erect sword fern, has long fronds with numerous, toothed pinnae. It likes indirect light with the compost kept moist at all times, unless the temperature drops. If this happens the plant should be allowed to dry out between watering. Nephrolepis prefers a peat-based compost and can be grown in a pot or a hanging basket. In ideal conditions it can grow to a substantial size. You could also consider Nephrolepis exaltata, Boston fern, which has many cultivars with feathery or ruffled edges.

Pteris cretica, the Cretan brake, also has long fronds but they are more ribbon-like. It needs the same conditions as nephrolepis. There are a number of varieties, some with the fronds deeply cut and other variegated forms with bands of white. If the tips turn brown either mist the foliage or stand the pot on damp gravel.

Adiantum raddianum, the maidenhair fern, also needs to be shielded from direct sun and prefers warm conditions. It is one of the most beautiful of all ferns with triangular delicate fronds. There are many forms, which differ in scale, colour and general shape but they all droop gracefully as they mature. Maidenhead ferns need humid conditions to grow well. Place them on a saucer filled with stones.

8.19

Fig. 8.18 There are
numerous cultivars
of *Pteris cretica*. Many
of them can be
propagated by spores.

Fig. 8.19 The Urn
plant (*Aechmea
fasciata*) flowers when
it is three to four
years old. The plant
dies after flowering
but produces off-
shoots, which can be
potted on to produce
new plants.

Fig. 8.20 Hippeastrums should need little introduction. If you water them regularly after flowering and feed them they will produce flowers during the following year. This variety is called 'Dawn White'.

Fig. 8.21 *Veltheimia bracteata* is a bulbous perennial with pink and white flowers.

Fig. 8.22 Maidenhair ferns need to be protected from direct sunlight. Provide them with a humid environment and they will reward you with profuse amounts of delicate green foliage.

Fig. 8.23 The Boston fern (*Nephrolepis exaltata*) looks wonderful in a shaded conservatory.

BROMELIADS

Aechmea fasciata, the urn plant, has a rosette of green leaves striped with grey, pink and blue flowers. It is widely available and easily grown. It is also worthwhile looking out for the many other beautiful species of aechmea. Like most bromeliads they like bright light. As far as watering is concerned all they need is for the water in the urn to be kept topped up and occasional fertilizer given to the compost and the urn. The flower is very long-lived but, once it has died down, small **offshoots** will appear around the base. These can be potted up in a peat-based compost, with grit or sand added for drainage, or in orchid compost. In two or three years you will once again be rewarded with their spectacular flowers.

Vriesea splendens, flaming swords, has loose rosettes of dark green leaves with brown bands. From these emerge the flattened spikes with small yellow tubular flowers and bright red bracts. It is again worth looking for other species which have different coloured markings on the leaves and yellow or bi-coloured bracts. *Vriesea hieroglyphica,* which is often called 'King of the bromeliads', is particularly striking. It has broad yellow-green leaves with bands of greenish-brown. Care is the same as for aechmea, although they prefer a minimum temperature of 15°C (59°F). No offsets are formed but they can be repotted after flowering.

BULBS

All the spring bulbs that can be grown in the house will flourish even more in a garden room with better light. This is also the case with hippeastrums, commonly called amaryllis. The flowers will last longer in a garden room, and if you plant the bulbs at intervals from late winter onwards they will provide colour for several months.

Veltheimia bracteata produces a spike of pink and white flowers in spring, from a rosette of glossy, green leaves. They like a light position and a high potash fertilizer until the flower appears. After flowering, continue feeding until the leaves turn yellow. Then, cut off the foliage and allow them to rest before repotting in late winter. Add plenty of sand to the compost and put a layer of crocks at the base of the pot.

Cyrtanthus elatus, Scarborough lily, is a relation of amaryllis but with much smaller flowers. It produces up to ten bright scarlet flowers on a stem. They do not need a rest period and can be kept growing in the same pot for several years.

Nerine sarniensis, Guernsey lily, will give you heads of pink flowers in the autumn. They should be potted in compost with some added sand in late summer with the tips at the surface. They should then be watered well until the leaves die down in late spring and left dry until early autumn. They can be put outside for this rest and will not need repotting for several years.

HANGING PLANTS

Begonia sutherlandii, with pale green leaves and bright orange flowers throughout the year, is an ideal plant for a hanging basket. All it needs is some shade from direct summer sun, regular feeding with a high potash fertilizer and plenty of water when it is growing.

Streptocarpus saxorum will also produce flushes of flowers throughout the year. The oval, velvety leaves are grey-green and the flowers pale violet. It can tolerate medium light at all times and cool conditions. Feed and water as above. Pot in a well-drained mixture.

SEASONAL PLANTING

As well as your choice of permanent plants for your garden room you can also import plants to provide colour at different times of the year. Most of the common house plants will welcome the better light and reward you with long-lasting flowers. In the winter, cyclamens will flower for months and in the summer there are the many varieties of streptocarpus in flower. There is even a new variety of streptocarpus called 'Blue Ice' which (it is claimed) will flower all year.

Fig. 8.24 Streptocarpus are quite easy plants and they produce quite beautiful flowers.

Fig. 8.25 The Scarborough lily has dramatic bright scarlet flowers. It prefers to be slightly pot bound.

Fig. 8.27 There are more than 2,000 species of bromeliad. One of the best for the conservatory is *Vriesea splendens*, other wise known as 'flaming swords'.

Fig. 8.26 *Begonia sutherlandii* is a tuberous begonia with delicate orange flowers. It has a very long flowering period.

9

THE CONSERVATORY
FOR PLANTS AND PEOPLE

Many people want their conservatory to be a place to sit or enjoy meals in a pleasant environment, where they also have the pleasure of growing some interesting exotic plants. This means making some compromises on comfort, with tiled floors rather than carpets, but it is still possible to use some hard-wearing rugs. However, simpler furniture will be needed than in a garden room – the kind that will not suffer from the odd drop of water. A larger number of plants means more dead leaves and petals to be cleared up.

Whether the conservatory will be used to sit in throughout the year or only from spring to autumn will determine the minimum temperature that has to be maintained in winter. This will influence which plants can be grown successfully. Many plants need or tolerate chilly winters provided the temperature does not fall below 7–10°C (45–50°F); but this will not provide a place for you to relax in. Alternatively, if you want to spend more time in the conservatory – in all but the coldest weather – then a minimum of 13–16°C (55–61°F) would be more comfortable. This can make it possible to grow some more demanding plants as well as many of those suitable for a cool conservatory, although many of the latter would need to be moved to a cooler place for a winter rest.

Finally, if a minimum temperature of 18–24°C (64–75°F) can be maintained, you could consider growing some tropical exotics. If you decide to do this you should remember that the room will not be very confortable to sit in, because of the high humidity that most of these plants require. Do remember that these minimum temperatures have to be maintained throughout the night, even though you will be in a warm house. It is also worth bearing in mind that it is very expensive to maintain this type of temperature. It only takes one night of cold weather to damage your plants.

Whatever the temperature you choose there will be room for some architectural plants to provide focal points for your display. Allow some plants to grow to their full height, it will change your conservatory from being a room with a few houseplants to an indoor garden.

The plants suggested in this chapter all add interest to a conservatory. Where they have a definite requirement for a minimum temperature of over 7°C (45°F), or a winter rest, this is mentioned. Some need bright light, others may require shade. You could also consider the plants that were described in the previous chapter. Consider having at least one lemon or orange, which will give you scent, flowers and fruit.

Previous page
Fig. 9.1 *Episcia cupreata* 'Silver Queen' needs high humidity if it is to do well. It spreads quickly by stolons.

Fig. 9.2 Given the right conditions bougainvillea can grow very quickly. It responds well to pruning and can be trained around a trellis. This is *B. glabra* 'Alexandria'.

Fig. 9.3 Norfolk Island Pine (*Araucaria heterophylla*) can reach a height of 60m (200ft) in the wild. In a pot it is unlikely to exceed 1.8m (6ft).

109

Fig. 9.4 The jelly palm, *Butia capitata*, has edible fruit. These can be used to make jam or jelly. It needs good light.

Fig. 9.5 The banana *Musa acuminata* 'Dwarf Cavendish' is widely cultivated in the Canary Islands. If you can keep it warm enough perhaps you'll be blessed with bananas!

STRUCTURAL PLANTS

Araucaria heterophylla, Norfolk Island pine, has tiers of branches covered with bright green pine-like leaves. It is easy to care for, needs medium light and repotting in soil-based compost every two to three years. The only disadvantage is that it may grow too fast but, with its roots restricted in a pot, it will be some time before it outgrows the available space and during that time it makes a very fine specimen plant, tolerant of a south-facing conservatory.

Ensete ventricosum, Abyssinian banana, is an easy and spectacular plant with huge, paddle-shaped leaves. All it needs is space, good light and lots of water – it can even go outside in summer. There is also a red-leafed variety called 'Maurelii'. An alternative banana is *Musa acuminata* 'Dwarf Cavendish' which likes hot, humid conditions and, in the right conditions, may even produce fruit. Another small banana with a wonderful flower is *Musa velutina.*

Ficus deltoidea, mistletoe fig, would be a good choice where space is more limited. It forms a neat bush with leaves that

are bright green above and brownish below. It bears small, yellow fruits all year. It prefers warmer temperatures, some shade in summer and care should be taken not to overwater it, especially in winter, as it grows slowly.

Butia capitata, the jelly palm, is an unusual palm with curved, feathery, blue-green leaves. It likes good light, well-drained, soil-based compost and plenty of water. It makes a good choice with grey-leafed plants.

Dypsis lutescens, golden cane palm, is colourful with long, arching, green leaves with yellow petioles. It is easy to care for, only needing plenty of water and bright, indirect light. *Dypsis decaryi,* triangle palm, with a triangular growth habit and silvery grey leaves is an alternative. It prefers moist, soil-based compost, but needs only a minimum of feeding.

Brugmansia sp., angel's trumpets, are a group of wonderful exotic plants with large, trumpet-shaped flowers. B. × *candida* 'Knightii' has 22–25cm (9–10in), white, fragrant flowers; B. × *candida* has fragrant, apricot-coloured flowers; and B. *sanguinea* with orange-red, unscented flowers are just a few to

Fig. 9.6 The Japanese banana, *Musa basjoo*, is the hardiest of the genus and is sometimes used outdoors as an exotic-looking bedding plant.

Fig. 9.7 Angel's trumpets (*Brugmansia* ✕ *candida*) is a large plant and can grow to a height of 1.8m (6ft) in a container. But take care – all parts of the plant are poisonous.

9.8

9.9

Fig. 9.11 The bleeding heart vine *Clerodendron thomsoniae*, has dense clusters of white and red flowers. It needs humus-rich, well-drained soil and good light.

Fig. 9.9 Bougainvillea is a flamboyant climber, which will brighten up any wall. This pink variety is *Bougainvillea* 'Barbara Karst'.

Fig. 9.8 *Agave americana* is a wonderful architectural plant, but it has lethal leaves. In Mexico it is planted as a very effective hedge.

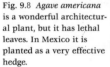

9.10

Fig. 9.10 *Clystoma callistegioides* is a rapidly growing climber with lavender-coloured flowers. These quickly fade to pale pink.

look for. With copious water and feeding you will be rewarded with flowers all year. If they get too big, they can be cut right back to the main stem in spring. They can also be put outside in summer to give the patio an exotic look. There is only one warning: all parts of the plant are poisonous, and it is wise to rinse your hands after touching them.

Agave americana, century plant, would be a good choice if you want a spiky specimen. It has rosettes of leaves, grey or grey-blue in colour, but varieties are available with white or yellow stripes down the leaves. They are again easy to grow as long as they have enough light and you avoid overwatering. Thought should be given as to where they should be placed, because of the sharp tips of the leaves. *A. filifera,* by contrast, has long, narrow, green leaves with thread-like edging.

CLIMBERS

Bougainvillea is a splendid plant, giving months of colour as long as it can be given direct sunlight. It should be pruned lightly after each flush of flowers. Prune hard in early spring and repot in John Innes No 3, with added grit or perlite. Allow the plant to dry out between watering – even during the summer months – and keep it very dry in winter, as this will encourage flowering. Only repot once the roots have completely filled the pot, as being slightly **pot-bound** also encourages flowering.

Jasminum sambac, Arabian jasmine, is an evergreen climber with white, very fragrant flowers. It will keep flowering in winter if the temperature is 10°C (50°F) or more. It likes to

9.11

grow in full sun, in a large pot and requires little pruning as it is slow-growing.

Hibbertia scandens, Guinea flower, is another evergreen climber with glossy leaves and bright yellow flowers. It also likes good light and needs to be kept warm all year. It grows best in a large pot but can be kept compact by pruning hard in the spring. It flowers all summer.

Philodendron scandens, the sweetheart plant, has glossy, heart-shaped leaves and is a plant for a shady position. It needs a minimum temperature of 16°C (61°F) and prefers a peat-based compost. Mist the leaves in hot weather, because this is a plant which prefers humid conditions, although it is generally an easy one to grow. You can train it around a moss-

covered pole where, given ideal conditions, it may grow to a considerable height.

Rhodochiton atrosanguineus, purple bell vine, has pinkish foliage and dark red flowers, which are produced well into winter. Even if it does not show signs of dying back it is best to cut it back around Christmas so it can start to grow again in spring. It is easily grown from seed.

Clerodendron thomsoniae, bleeding heart vine, is a vigorous evergreen climber with clusters of white and red flowers from late summer into winter. It will cover a wall. It prefers warm conditions, but care is needed with watering to avoid the soil getting saturated. After flowering it should be kept dry for a few weeks to encourage flowering the following year.

9.16

9.17

Fig. 9.12 *Pittosporum tobira* 'Variegatum' has orange blossom-scented flowers.

Fig. 9.13 *Brunfelsia pauciflora* 'Macrantha' has fragrant purple flowers with a white centre.

Fig. 9.14 Formerly known as coleus, the leaves of solenostemon are vivid combinations of red, green, yellow and pink.

Fig. 9.15 *Melianthus major* is grown mainly for it stunning foliage.

Fig. 9.16 *Pavonia multiflora* is a small shrub with bright red flowers.

Fig. 9.17 The bright scarlet flowers of the New Zealand christmas tree can't help but attract attention.

Clytostoma callistegioides, trumpet vine, is a slender climber with white, violet-shaded flowers in spring and summer. It is evergreen with two long leaflets and a tendril. It is suitable for cool conditions and prefers good light. It can be pruned after flowering or in early spring.

FOLIAGE PLANTS

Pittosporum tobira 'Variegatum' forms a compact bush with cream and green leaves and with the added advantage of white, scented flowers in summer. It needs a free-draining compost so add grit or perlite and allow it to dry out between waterings.

Pseudopanax lessonii 'Gold Splash' has striking gold, variegated leaves, another cultivar 'Purpureus' has purple foliage. They are very easy plants needing minimum care and good light in winter, but need some shade in summer.

Melianthus major, honey bush, has long grey-green leaves with crinkled edges and is an easy foliage plant in shade or brighter light. It can be trained to grow up a pillar.

Corynocarpus laevigatus is a strong plant for sun or shade and is a good choice if you like green and white variation. It is an attractive, bushy plant with white tips to the leaves and also produces small, greenish-yellow flowers in summer. They may ripen to give edible, orange berries but the seeds they contain are extremely poisonous.

Stromanthe sanguinea is a good choice if you want a low-growing, foliage plant to grow under a tall, structural plant. It has large, glossy, pale green leaves which have dark green markings and a purple undersurface. It prefers medium light and warm conditions with good humidity.

Formerly known as coleus, *Solenostemon* hybrids, or flame nettles, come in a bewildering choice of leaf colours. The most exotic plants can be obtained from a specialist supplier, they can even be pruned to form a standard. They like good light, to be well fed and watered in spring and summer.

Acalypha wilkesiana, copperleaf, is available in several named varieties with green, orange or red foliage. It can grow to 2m (6½ft) in height but in a pot it is possible to keep it smaller. It prefers warm conditions, but will tolerate a minimum temperature of 10°C (50°F) in winter if it is allowed to become dormant, by giving it just enough water to keep it alive. The leaves will drop but it will revive in spring. *Acalypha* should be cut back by about two thirds once growth starts again.

Fig. 9.18 *Senna corymbosa* is a member of the pea family and has racemes of bright golden-yellow flowers.

Fig. 9.19 *Alyogyne huegelii* has stunning satin-textured lavender-mauve flowers. It can have as many as 30-40 flowers on a plant at a time.

FLOWERING PLANTS

Brunfelsia pauciflora, yesterday-today-and-tomorrow, has scented flowers, which are produced from summer into autumn; they start mauve and then fade to white. It should be given good light and kept dry during the winter, but watered freely when growing. Pot in John Innes No 2 and prune back by half in early spring.

Justicia carnea, king's crown, has large, upright, pink flower heads in summer and dark green foliage. It is important to deadhead to encourage repeated flushes of flowers. Give them good light and fertilize well when growing; prune back hard after flowering has stopped.

Pavonia multiflora is a slow-growing, upright shrub with crimson and purple flowers all year. It thrives in warm,

9.19

sunny conditions but tolerates 10°C (50°F) in winter. It likes rich compost which should be kept moist at all times. Prune back in spring to avoid it getting too tall and to encourage new shoots.

Metrosideros excelsa, New Zealand christmas tree, has attractive greyish foliage and brilliant scarlet flowers. It flowers in early summer and can then be put outside until autumn. During the winter keep it cool until growth starts in spring. Use ericaceous compost as it likes acidity. *M. kermadecensis* 'Variegatus' is similar but has variegated foliage.

Alyogyne huegelii flowers for most of the year. It has large lavender-mauve flowers and the plant can be put outside to flower on a patio during the summer. To make sure it continues flowering remember to deadhead it, keep it well watered and fed.

Cestrum roseum 'Ilnacullin' grows into a small bush with bright pink flowers in summer and winter. It grows best in soil-based compost and should be cut back in spring or it will get straggly. *Cestrum* 'Newellii' has crimson flowers.

Globba winitii, has unusual, pendant, purple flowers in autumn which consist of purple bracts from which emerge small, yellow flowers. Light shade, warmth and humidity suit them and they complement foliage plants which have purple leaves. They will die down in winter, when they should be kept just moist.

Senna corymbosa is an easy, vigorous, evergreen shrub with yellow flowers in summer and attractive, divided leaves. It will grow to 2m (6½ft) in height, but it can be pruned if you want a smaller plant. Another species with large, conspicuous flowers is *S. didymobotrya.*

FERNS

Asplenium nidus, the bird's nest fern, has a rosette of bright
green, glossy leaves. It likes good, indirect light but can cope
with shade. It is most successful in a warm conservatory,
where a minimum temperature of 15°C (59°F) can be
maintained. To grow well it needs good humidity, which will
prevent the edges of the fronds turning brown. The compost
should be moist at all times. If the fronds are damaged they
can be cut right back to the base in spring.

Davallia canariensis, hare's foot fern, with its feathery
fronds and furry, horizontal stem (which does indeed look
remarkably like a hare's foot), can be grown in a pot, in a bed
under other plants, or in a hanging basket. It is a tolerant
fern needing only shade and the compost to be kept moist.

BROMELIADS

Guzmania, scarlet star, is listed in catalogues as varieties
rather than the species, which can be hard to find. They produce their flowers, which are surrounded by brightly
coloured bracts, in the centre of a rosette of bright green
leaves. The bracts, which are mostly red, remain colourful for
many weeks during the autumn and winter. They grow best
in a minimum temperature of 15°C (59°F) with some shade
from direct sun. Keep the cup in the centre topped up with
water, ideally rainwater, unless the temperature falls below
15°C (59°F). Feed with diluted fertilizer every third watering.
Use peat-based compost, mixed with coarse sand when
repotting in spring.

Neoregelia carolinae, blushing bromeliad, is similar but the
central leaves are coloured, surrounding small, purple
flowers. Care is as described above, although it will tolerate
lower temperatures.

BULBS

Clivia miniata, kaffir lily, has a whorl of dark green leaves
from which comes a stem with large, orange flowers in winter or early spring. If you plant it in a pot it can be moved to
a less conspicuous position after flowering, but it can also be
planted in a bed where it will produce many flowers at the
same time. Pot clivias in John Innes No 2, keep them slightly
pot-bound and well-fed. The bulbs are poisonous.

Curcuma alismatifolia has unusual three-petalled, cone-like
flowers, which are borne on erect stems. It flowers in the
summer and has pale mauve or rose-pink blooms. It is best
planted in a soil-based compost, with some added grit to

Fig. 9.20 The bird's nest
fern (*Asplenium nidus*)
can grow very large if it
is provided with the cor-
rect conditions.

Fig. 9.21 Guzmania
hybrids can be found in
a wide range of vivid
colours.

Fig. 9.22 Kaffir lilies (*Clivia miniata*) are long-lived plants, but they need a winter rest if you want them to flower well.

Fig. 9.23 *Neoregalia carolinae* 'White Parade' is a striking bromeliad with green and white striped leaves.

Fig. 9.24 Calla lilies thrive in a conservatory. They come from South Africa and make an elegant and striking addition to a room.

improve the drainage. It should be allowed to die down after flowering and should be stored in a dry, cool place.

Habranthus robustus, is a smaller relation of the well-known hippeastrum with pink flowers in early autumn. Pot them in spring and then leave them for several years to become crowded together before repotting.

Zantedeschia aethiopica, calla lily, looks spectacular in a conservatory with its large, shining, green leaves and pure white flowers on long stalks. Bulbs should be planted in autumn just below the surface, in soil-based compost and kept just moist until growth starts. They then need warmth, liberal watering and bright light – they will flower from mid-winter onwards. During the summer they can stand outside and be allowed to become dormant until the next autumn. There are a number of varieties: one, which is called 'Green Goddess', has a green-flushed spathe. The sap of this plant is poisonous.

HANGING PLANTS

Episcia dianthiflora, the lace-flower vine, with its furry, green leaves and fringed white flowers is an attractive plant for a hanging basket. It can also be grown as ground cover between tall plants. It does need a minimum of 13°C (55°F) in winter, bright light and to be kept moist and humid. Although this may make it appear demanding to grow, it is a very attractive plant. There is also *E. cupreata,* with orange flowers and coppery leaves.

Lotus berthelotii, coral gem or parrot's beak, has silvery leaves and scarlet flowers from spring onwards. It needs good light but is otherwise undemanding, although using a high potash fertilizer will help it to keep flowering.

SEASONAL PLANTING

Just as in a garden, added colour and interest can be created at different times of the year in a conservatory. Spring bulbs will come into flower early, lilies in a pot will give fragrance and flowering houseplants, such as azaleas, will find the conditions in a conservatory much more favourable.

The conservatory gives you the opportunity to grow a range of plants that would never survive indoors as house plants. While a greenhouse can create ideal growing conditions a conservatory represents a good compromise and will allow you to grow a range of exotic plants.

CHAPTER **10**

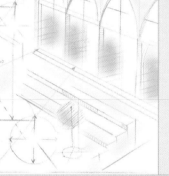

WHEN PLANTS
COME FIRST

I f you are willing to put the needs of your plants first and give them enough time and attention, then the choice of what you can grow is bewildering. You will almost certainly have some ideas about which type of plants you want to grow. It may be plants with tropical foliage that attract you, or the diverse shapes of cacti and succulents. You may want flowers and scent all year round or perhaps wish to grow some unusual fruit.

The first thing to consider is what will be the minimum temperature you are going to be able to maintain during the winter. A cool conservatory will allow you to choose from a wide range of plants but if you want the spectacular foliage of alocasia or the scent of a gardenia you should aim for a minimum temperature of 18°C (64°F). If you are willing to accept some losses it is always worth trying to grow a plant at a lower temperature than is recommended. Anthuriums are a good example; while they are often said to need a minimum temperature of 16°C (61°F) they will grow well in a cool conservatory, as long as they are kept fairly dry in winter.

Humidity is another factor. If plants are to come first then, unless cacti and succulents are your choice, being able to maintain reasonable humidity by damping down the floor in hot weather will make for success.

As well as the plants in this chapter, some of which may need more care and attention or are more demanding in their conditions for growth, the plants in the earlier chapters can be added to your collection.

Previous page
Fig. 10.1 The king protea, *Protea cyanaroides*, is a dramatic shrub with deep pink or crimson bracts. It needs very well-drained compost.

Fig. 10.2 The shuttle-cock protea, *Protea aurea*, can grow to a height of 5m (16ft) in the wild. This is the variety 'Goodwood Red'.

Fig. 10.3 The bird of paradise makes an excellent plant for the conservatory. It is relatively easy to grow from seed, but may take as long as six years before it flowers.

Fig. 10.4 Given the
correct growing condi-
tions the sago palm
(*Cycas revoluta*) will
eventually develop a
substantial trunk.

STRUCTURAL PLANTS

Cupressus cashmeriana, Kashmir cypress is a beautiful tree from the foothills of the Himalayas. It has long, pendant branches of greyish-blue foliage and can grow to a considerable height outdoors. Planted in John Innes No 3, with good light, watering and feeding, it makes a wonderful specimen plant. To avoid it becoming too big it may be better to grow it in a large pot rather than a bed. It grows quite slowly so it does not need pruning.

Strelitzia reginae, the bird of paradise flower, produces spectacular flowers and bold foliage. A warm conservatory is recommended but it will grow in cool conditions. If you are growing it from seed it may be several years before it flowers. However, when it does, you will get a real sense of achievement. Once it is mature do not repot as root restriction helps flowering. Grow in good light in a large pot of John Innes No 3 or in a border. *S. nicolai* has white flowers, but it is a much larger plant.

Sparrmannia africana, African hemp, has huge, hairy leaves and clusters of white flowers in winter. It usually starts flowering in mid-winter and goes on until spring. It can then be pruned hard and moved to a less conspicuous place until the following year, although the leaves are still attractive. It is a very easy plant to grow with normal care but feed well in the summer to encourage flowering.

Cycas revoluta, the sago palm, is very decorative with a whorl of feathery leaves on top of a swollen base. It must have good light but is otherwise very tolerant. Use soil-based compost with added sand or perlite to give good drainage and allow the top 2cm (¾in) to dry out between each watering. Young plants may produce only one new leaf per year, but mature specimens may produce a dozen or more. It can go outside in summer.

Yucca aloifolia, Spanish bayonet, has a single trunk, on top of which are tufts of long, dark blue-green leaves with sharp points. They must have several hours of sun each day and should be grown in a clay pot in soil-based compost. This will reduce the risk of them being knocked over; they are heavy plants. It is also important that they are placed where no one will injure themselves on the sharp leaf tips. Water sparingly in winter. They can be left outside during the summer months. Other species to consider are *Y. whipplei,* which is smaller with narrow, grass-like leaves and can tolerate shade; *Y. filamentosa* which has long stalks of white flowers; and *Yucca elephantipes.* This last species is larger but its leaves do not have sharp points.

Aloe arborescens, candelabra plant, is another plant to consider if you want a spiky effect. Like all aloes it is extremely easy to grow. It has a loose rosette of grey-green leaves with saw edges and tall, red flowers. There is also *A. vera,* the medicine plant, deriving its common name from the healing

Fig. 10.5 Adam's needle (*Yucca filamentosa*) produces large spikes of white flowers. The Latin name is derived from the way in which the margins of the leaves split to produce thin filaments.

Fig. 10.6 *Aloe arborescens* is a fast-growing succulent which can form a substantial bush in a conservatory.

Fig. 10.7 The screw pine, *Pandanus ultilis*, comes from Madagascar. In the wild it forms a substantial tree, but it can be kept small in a conservatory.

Fig. 10.8 Mimose de quatre saisons (*Acacia retinodes*) has numerous greyish-green leaves. It produces racemes of globe-shaped golden-yellow flowers.

property of the jelly interior when used for burns or bruises. They are very tolerant plants, although the spiny leaves of both species again necessitate taking precautions against injury. All aloes like good light and a dry, winter rest.

Pandanus utilis, screw pine, can grow to a height of 20m (65ft) outside, but indoors it will probably only attain a height of 1-2 m (3–6ft). It has spiny-edged leaves arranged spirally around a corkscrew-shaped trunk. Once again it has to be in a safe place because of the spines. Indirect light, a minimum winter temperature of 16°C (61°F) and summer misting will encourage it to grow.

Ficus lyrata, fiddle-leaf fig, has fiddle-shaped leaves, as its name suggests. The large leaves are dark green and glossy with paler veins. It will grow into a small tree with branches all round so it does need some space. With light shade, some warmth, plenty of feeding, watering and summer misting it will grow into an exotic foliage plant. It can be pruned in spring or the tips of the branches can be cut off to produce a bushy plant.

Brahea armata, Mexican blue palm, is the palm to choose if your colour scheme demands blue foliage. It has fan-shaped leaves growing from a short trunk. It tolerates dry air and cold conditions but needs bright light. Well worth growing.

Caryota mitis, the fishtail palm, is another interesting palm with fishtail-shaped leaves. Although it prefers good, indirect light it will tolerate low light but needs warmth and humidity. It grows slowly so it will be many years before it gets too big for your conservatory.

Fig. 10.10 *Acacia baileyana*, cootamundra wattle, is a small tree with arching branches. It bears dense racemes of golden-yellow flowers.

Fig. 10.9 *Cyathea australis* is a tall elegant tree fern. It grows most luxuriously in half shade.

Fig. 10.11 The fishtail palm (*Caryota mitis*) is slow-growing and tolerant of low light conditions.

Licuala grandis, ruffled fan palm, has some of the most beautiful fronds of any palm. They are about 60cm (24in) in diameter, circular and pleated. It is quite a demanding palm, requiring both good humidity and warmth. Easier to grow, because it is less fussy about humidity, is *L. spinosa* with tougher, split leaves.

Cyathea australis, rough tree fern, has a circle of huge fronds growing from the top of the trunk. Like all ferns it prefers shade, although it will tolerate some sun, and, as it is slow-growing, it will take many years before it gets too big. John Innes No 3 is recommended. *C. dealbata* has silvery undersides to the leaves.

Acacia retinodes is a mimosa with narrow, willow-like leaves and fragrant, yellow flowers from winter onwards. This is in contrast to the other species of the genus, which are spring-flowering. It will grow rapidly into a small tree, so it is really a plant for the larger conservatory. It can, however, be kept in check by hard pruning after flowering. To stimulate flowering it is important to keep it cool, the compost must be moist (even in winter) and it should be given plenty of high phosphate fertilizer. It can be left outside in the summer. There are also many spring-flowering species to consider, such as *A. dealbata,* which is the florists' mimosa, or *A. baileyana* (cootamundra wattle).

CLIMBERS

Stephanotis floribunda, Madagascar jasmine, has heavily scented white flowers throughout the summer. It can be trained across the roof so that the flowers hang down. Its reputation

10.12

10.13

10.15

10.14

Fig. 10.12 *Stephanotis floribunda* can be quite difficult to grow, but its flowers have a most wonderful fragrance.

Fig. 10.13 *Allamanda schottii*, the bush allamanda, has deep golden-yellow flowers with orange-red streaks on the inside.

Fig. 10.14 *Rosa banksiae* 'Lutea' is a vigorous climbing rose, with few thorns. The double flowers are yellow and slightly fragrant.

Fig. 10.15 *Lapageria rosea var* 'Albiflora' is a white form of the Chilean bellflower.

Fig. 10.16 *Pyrostegia venusta* is an attractive climbing plant with tubular orange flowers.

Fig. 10.17 The rose grape, *Medinilla magnifica*, has large glossy leaves and enormous panicles of pale pink flowers.

Fig. 10.18 *Phoenix roebelenii* is a small date palm, which is perfect for the conservatory.

as being difficult to grow is undeserved, since all it needs is a minimum temperature of 10–13°C (50–55°F), good light (but without direct sun) and ericaceous compost. It should be given a cool, dry winter rest.

Gloriosa superba 'Rothschildiana' has exotic, spidery, red flowers with yellow margins in late summer and autumn. They are wonderful plants but they do need a temperature of 22°C (72°F) for growth, plus light shade. After flowering, continue to water until the plants die off. You can leave the tubers in their pot or store them dry in a warm place at about 17°C (63°F). It is another poisonous plant, and the tubers can cause skin irritation.

Tetrastigma voinierianum, chestnut vine, is a rapidly growing, evergreen climber which can be used to grow over the roof of a conservatory to give some shade or to screen an ugly view. It has large leaves like those of a horse chestnut – hence the name. As you would expect from such a rapidly growing plant it needs a rich compost such as John Innes No 3. It tolerates some shade and needs lots of water to maintain all the lush foliage. It is best pruned hard.

Allamanda cathartica, golden trumpet, is another evergreen but with the added attraction of golden, trumpet-shaped flowers from summer to autumn. It prefers a warm conservatory but is well worth trying in cooler conditions. Cut out the old flowering shoots in winter as next year's flowers will be borne on the new shoots growing up from the base. It should be given a dry, winter rest. Yet another poisonous plant.

Pyrostegia venusta, flame flower, is very spectacular with many clusters of orange flowers from late autumn onwards. It is evergreen and can be trained over the roof of a warm conservatory to allow the flowers to hang down. It needs direct sunlight to flower and a few weeks' dry rest after flowering.

Hardenbergia violacea is another winter-flowering climber with deep violet-blue flowers. It is suitable for a cool conservatory. It likes good light and should be cut back after flowering. If it is planted beside a summer-flowering climber you will have flowers all year.

Lapageria rosea, Chilean bell flower, has pink flowers in late summer and autumn and leathery, green leaves. It must have cool conditions, shade in summer and well-drained, lime-free soil. You should use rainwater to water it if you live in a hard water area. *Lapageria* is an evergreen perennial which does not need pruning. It can be difficult to grow but if you are successful it is a spectacular sight when it is in flower. It is a good idea to add some charcoal to the compost.

Fig. 10.19 'Muscat of Alexandria' is one of the best dessert grapevines It is late-ripening but produces gorgeous, golden-yellow, aromatic grapes.

Fig. 10.20 'Black Hamburg' is a late-ripening grapevine for producing wine. It can be grown in a greenhouse or conservatory.

Rosa banksiae 'Lutea' is a beautiful, slightly scented, yellow rose which is best grown in a conservatory. You will find it a truly wonderful sight in early spring, long before there are any signs of roses in the garden. Deadhead the plant regularly in order to prolong flowering, and prune it lightly after flowering has stopped. It is best to use rose fertilizer. Another favourite is 'Marechal Niel'; which is even more fragrant and resistant to disease.

Mitraria coccinea, Chilean mitre flower, is a much smaller, more delicate climber that should flower from spring to autumn. The flowers are small, but they are very numerous and bright orange or red. In fine contrast, the evergreen leaves are glossy and coarsely toothed. It will grow in semi-shade and cool conditions.

Vitis vinifera, grapevines, need considerable care and proper pruning if they are to be successful in the conservatory. Some varieties can be grown in pots but one recommended method, if you remember to tell your builder in time, is to plant it just outside the base wall and bring the stem through a small hole in the wall. There are many varieties available: some are black, some green, and they vary in the time that the fruit ripen. It is best to consult a specialist supplier and discuss with them which variety would be most suitable for your conditions.

Senecio tamoides, Portuguese geranium, is another winter-flowering climber with scented, yellow, daisy-like flowers from late autumn onwards. It is evergreen with ivy-shaped leaves. It grows fast and will need pruning after flowering in spring, but otherwise it just needs normal care. Like all winter-flowering plants, feeding and watering should continue while they are growing.

10.20

Fig. 10.21 The 'giant elephant's ear' (*Alocasia macrorrhiza*) is well worth growing if you have the space. It requires a high temperature and regular misting.

Fig. 10.22 *Thunbergia mysorensis* is a shrubby climber with long pendant racemes of yellow and reddish-brown flowers. It originally came from India.

Thunbergia grandiflora, blue trumpet vine, is a reliable, tall climber with large, beautiful, blue flowers in summer. It prefers warm conditions and can be pruned right back in spring if it is getting too big. Alternatively the main stems can be allowed to grow up over the roof.

FOLIAGE PLANTS

Alocasia macrorrhiza, giant elephant's ear, is one of the most spectacular of all foliage plants. It has large, arrow-shaped leaves with lovely markings. It needs warmth and humidity however, so it's only worth considering if you have the right conditions. A minimum temperature of 18°C (64°F) is recommended and frequent damping down to maintain humidity. They grow best in a peaty mixture and need shade from direct sun. There is also a variegated variety.

Philodendron melanochyrsum has slightly smaller leaves and is less demanding, although it still needs some warmth, with a minimum of 13°C (55°F), humidity and shade. There are several different species with different leaf colourings and markings. Although it can be grown as a climber, it makes an effective foliage plant if given some support or it can be used to underplant a large plant such as a banana.

Iresine herbstii, beefsteak plant, is much smaller, reaching only 60cm (24in) in height, with attractive maroon and crimson foliage. It needs light to develop the leaf colours and growing points should be nipped out in order to promote bushiness. There is also a variety, 'Aureoreticulata', with bright green leaves and red stems.

Ctenanthe lubbersiana is another smaller foliage plant with long, pointed, green leaves with paler markings, which can be grown in cool conditions with some shade.

Olea europaea, olives, have silvery grey foliage and tiny, yellow flowers in spring which, with good management, should ripen to produce olives. If they are picked green they need to be soaked before they are eaten. The secret is to add lime to the compost and use citrus fertilizer. They like well-drained compost that should be kept just moist all year. With careful pruning you can produce standards or any other shape you would like.

Ardisia crenata, coral berry, is an evergreen shrub with clusters of red berries at Christmas, which remain on the plant for many months. They need to be kept cool in winter with the compost moist at all times and benefit from misting with tepid water.

Fig. 10.23 *Philodendron bipinnatifidum* can grow to a height of 2m (6½ft). The leaves may measure as much as one metre in length and are deeply pinnate.

Fig. 10.24 *Iresine herbstii* has some unusual common names, including 'beefsteak plant', 'beef plant' and 'chicken gizzard'!

Fig. 10.25 Chinese taro, *Alocasia cucullata*, grows to a height of 1.5m (5ft) and has massive glossy green leaves.

Fig. 10.26 The bengal trumpet vine (*Thunbergia grandiflora*) is perhaps the most beautiful of all climbing plants. It has long racemes of mauve-blue flowers.

Cyperus involucratus, umbrella grass, needs to stand in water – so it is a good choice for the conservatory with a water feature. It forms a clump of umbrella-shaped foliage and is a tough, easy plant which prefers to be in full sun.

Coffea arabica, coffee, has glossy, green leaves and once established will flower and then bear red coffee beans. Unfortunately, you are unlikely to have enough to roast for your breakfast coffee but it is an attractive plant needing a minimum of 15°C (59°F) and good light.

FLOWERING PLANTS

Hedychium gardnerianum, the Kahili ginger lily, will grow up to 1.5m (5ft) with perfumed, yellow flowers in late summer and autumn. It has lovely foliage, rather reminiscent of a banana plant, and could be considered as a structural plant. In the growing season they like full sun, lots of water and fertilizer. They prefer cool conditions, and could be grown outside in the summer in a protected position, although they need to be brought in for the winter. There are several other species, including some with red flowers.

Impatiens niamniamensis, cockatoo plant, has beaked flowers of red, yellow and green. It has dark green foliage and will be in flower for most of the year. It is quite unlike its well known relations, the busy lizzies. It may get straggly so it can be cut back in spring.

Clerodendron × *speciosum* is an evergreen scrambler with clusters of red flowers from late summer to well into autumn. It needs space, so it is unsuitable for a small conservatory. Like the climbing species, it likes warm conditions and good light but needs some shade from direct sun. It will survive cooler conditions if it is kept fairly dry in winter.

Cuphea ignea, cigar flower, grows into a small, round, evergreen bush with bright orange, tubular flowers in summer. The only problem is that it may become straggly so it needs to be cut back hard in early winter. There is also *C. hyssopifolia* with cerise flowers.

Medinilla magnifica, rose grape, is a really exotic-looking plant with large bunches of pinkish-purple flowers hanging from the branches. These are produced in spring and usually again in autumn. To appreciate the flowers, the plant should be above eye level. It needs a minimum temperature of 18°C (64°F) and humidity. The warmer and more humid the conditions the better the display of flowers. As you might expect with such a rich-looking plant, it appreciates good feeding and is well worth all the care and attention.

Fig. 10.27 The coral-berry, *Ardisia crenata*, has white or pink flowers. It has coral-red to scarlet coloured berries.

Fig. 10.28 *Clerodendron* × *specisoum*, the Java glory bean, has pale red or pink flowers and dark green leaves. It may grow too big for a small conservatory.

Fig. 10.29 The coffee plant, *Coffea arabica*, has glossy dark green foliage. The fragrant white flowers appear in clusters. If you are lucky you might even be able to produce your own coffee.

Fig. 10.30 The Kahili ginger lily (*Hedychium gardnerianum*) can grow to a height of 1.5m (5ft) or more. It has spikes of yellow and white flowers.

10.30

Streptosolen jamesonii, marmalade bush, is, as the name suggests, a small, evergreen bush which is covered by vivid orange flowers for much of the year. It needs to be pruned in late winter and the tips pinched in summer to keep its shape, as it can get straggly. Alternatively it can be encouraged to grow as a climber.

Justicia rizzinii is a quite different plant from its relation J. carnea. It is winter-flowering with masses of red flowers with yellow tips. It will grow to 60cm (24in) with small, evergreen, downy leaves. It should be put outside for a rest in late summer/early autumn for the flower buds to ripen.

Kunzea baxteri is an Australian plant with small, dark green leaves and brilliant scarlet flowers. It comes from a dry area, so it requires good drainage and should be allowed to dry out before it is watered again.

Protea cynaroides, the king protea, is a large shrub with spectacular pink or cream flower heads in spring and early summer. Again, these plants dislike phosphates so care is needed with compost and fertilizing. A compost made up from peat or peat substitute, mixed with one third of grit,

would be ideal. You may have to wait a year or so for flowers but you will be rewarded by unusual and long-lasting blooms which can also be dried for flower arranging.

Asclepias curassavica, blood flower, will grow to about 1m (3ft) and has bright orange flowers with protruding yellow **stamens** in summer and autumn. It likes good light and even direct sun. It is poisonous however.

Heliconia 'Bucky' is an exotic banana relation with large leaves and orange-red **bracts** surrounding yellow-green flowers. It will grow faster in a warm conservatory but is remarkably tolerant of lower temperatures in winter if it is kept drier. The lower temperature may kill off the top growth and while it will probably produce new foliage there may be no flowers. It is best planted in a free-draining compost and plants should be well fed. H. bihai is larger and can reach 2m (6½ft). It has red bracts with yellow tips.

Rhododendron veitchianum Cubittii Group are a group of free-flowering rhododendrons which are ideally suited to growing in pots in a conservatory. They are best grown in a free-draining medium, such as orchid compost. They require

Fig. 10.31 (*far left*) Australia is the source of many wonderful conservatory plants. *Kunzea baxteri* is a medium-sized shrub that produces scarlet-red flowers.

Fig. 10.32 (*left*) The marmalade bush (*Streptosolen jamesonii*) has wonderful orange-yellow flowers. It originally came from Colombia and Peru.

Fig. 10.34 *Justicia rizzini* is a small rounded shrub with pretty clusters of nodding flowers. These are scarlet with yellow tips.

Fig. 10.33 The cigar flower, *Cuphea ignea*, is also known as the firecracker plant. It bears scarlet flowers in the summer and autumn.

very little fertilizer and dislike phosphate. They can be placed outside on the terrace during the summer. Many, such as *R. 'Fragrantissimum'*, are scented and you will find hybrids in a wide range of colours.

FERNS

Pellaea rotundifolia, button fern, is an attractive small fern with rounded leaflets which can be grown as ground cover in a bed or in the shade of a taller plant. The leaves may be slightly hairy underneath, so they don't like being splashed or sprayed with water.

Cyrtomium falcatum, holly fern, is another good fern for the cool conservatory. It has masses of glossy, holly-like fronds which grow to 30–60cm (12–24in). John Innes No 2 is a suitable compost.

Blechnum gibbum has a whorl of dark green fronds on top of a trunk, which can reach a height of 90cm (36in). It is a striking plant which can be used as a focal point in a display. It prefers a warm conservatory and acid compost. It can be grown in sun or shade.

10.35

Fig. 10.35 (*left*) *Heliconia rostrata* has striking bright red bracts, with yellow tips and green edges. They look like a series of birds' bills.

Fig. 10.36 (*right*) The blood flower, *Asclepias curassavica*, is a small shrub. It comes from tropical South America and has umbels of striking orange-red flowers.

10.36

10.37

Fig. 10.37 Some rho-
dendrons, such the
one illustrated (*R.
veitchianum* Cubitti
Group), are suitable
for growing in
the conservatory.

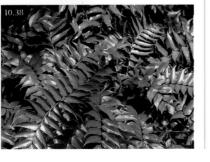

10.38

Fig. 10.38 The holly
fern is semi-hardy
and tolerates drier air
than most other ferns.
It has glossy, dark
green foliage.

Platycerium bifurcatum, stag horn fern, with its fronds forked
like a stag's antlers, is best grown attached to a piece of tree
bark. In nature it normally grows high up in the branches of
a tree, so it likes a good amount of light. The easiest way to
water it is to immerse it in a bucket of water. Wait until the
compost has nearly dried out and then leave it in the water
for about 15 minutes in the growing period or two minutes
during the rest period.

BROMELIADS

Ananas comosus, pineapple, makes an attractive feature with
its whorl of stiff, spiny leaves and, in the right conditions,
purple-blue flowers with red bracts will grow up in the centre
during the summer. After they fade you may even find that
you have a pineapple. The conditions you will need are very
bright light and a warm conservatory. Pineapples should be
grown in a well-drained compost with plenty of coarse bark in
it. There is also a variegated form with attractively striped
leaves and a smaller species, which is called *A. nana*.

139

Tillandsia cyanea, has a loose whorl of grey-green leaves from which emerges a fan-shaped flower head. It consists of overlapping pink bracts, which protect the bright blue flowers. These flowers last for two months or more. Warm conditions and regular misting is what they need. After flowering, the offsets which form around the old plant can be potted into a bromeliad compost. *T. usneoides,* Spanish moss, is completely different. It has thread-like stems, which are covered with minute, silvery leaves. These hang down in a tangled mass. It looks very effective when attached to an epiphyte tree.

BULBS

Hymenocallis × festalis, the spider lily, has narrow leaves and a group of white flowers with the petals divided into curling segments. The flowers are held on a 60cm (24in) high stem in spring. After the flowers die down they can be dried off and the bulbs stored until planted again from late autumn onwards. They grow well in a cool conservatory. *H. × macrostephana* is very similar.

Crinum moorei, swamp lily, produces pale pink or white, fragrant flowers in late summer. After flowering the bulbs need a dry rest, following which they can be replanted in spring in loam-based compost.

HANGING PLANTS

Aeschynanthus radicans, lipstick plant, is a trailing plant with fleshy leaves and tubular red flowers in summer. Care is needed as it dislikes draughts and fluctuations in temperature but, given the right conditions, the showy flowers provide an exotic display. They require misting in summer, shade from direct sun and need to be cut back after flowering. There is also a wide range of cultivars available, some with attractive orange flowers.

Columnea hybrids, goldfish plants, have brightly coloured red, orange or yellow flowers early in the year. Some have variegated foliage. They like a minimum temperature of 10°C (50°F) and dislike compost which is too damp, so they should be allowed to dry out between waterings. To grow well the humidity needs to be kept high by misting. After flowering they should be cut back and left fairly dry during the winter.

CACTI AND SUCCULENTS

Aeonium arboreum has whorls of dark green to purple, fleshy leaves at the end of twisted branches – making a truly architectural plant. Like all of this group, they prefer a loose and well-aerated compost. You can either make your own or buy

10.39

10.40

Fig. 10.39 The leaves of *Echeveria subrigida* have red edges and form neat rosettes. They need full sunshine and very well-drained soil.

Fig. 10.40 The stag horn fern is an epiphyte and is best grown attached to a piece of bark.

Fig. 10.41 The pineapple plant belongs to the bromeliad family. The variety 'Variegatus' has yellow striped leaves, with red edges.

compost which has been specially formulated for cacti. Cacti prefer good light and can tolerate low night temperatures – which they would be exposed to in their natural desert conditions – but they do need warmth during the day. Because they are slow-growing, fertilizer should be given at a quarter to half strength during the growing season. Allow them to become almost dry before watering, particularly in the winter when they will need very little attention. There are several varieties, offering a choice of leaf colour and size. Care is the same as for other members of this group.

Echeveria secunda var. *glauca,* has rosettes of large, pale blue leaves and little red and orange flowers in summer. You can find many different species and varieties of these plants varying in leaf shape, flower colour and size.

Opuntia phaeacantha, prickly pear, has yellow flowers and the flat, prickly leaves of this group. These are prostrate and eventually form a mat. Other species have the more typical upright habit and endow a conservatory with a real desert feel. It is another plant which you either like or would not dream of having.

Epiphyllum hybrids, orchid cactus, as the name suggests, has spectacular flowers. The plants have long, pale leaves and flowers in a range of fantastic colours in spring. They prefer semi-shade and free-draining compost but, unlike other cacti, the roots should be kept moist all year round.

ORCHIDS

Cymbidium hybrids are one of the most popular groups of orchids with long, strap-shaped leaves and decorative and long-lasting flowers. There are winter-, spring- and autumn-flowering varieties and standard- or miniature-sized plants. Flowers come in a wide range of colours with contrasting patterns on the lip. During the winter they need a cool conservatory, with good light. It is worth using a special orchid compost and an orchid fertilizer, which are available from garden centres. Give fertilizer at every second or third watering but also use it as a foliar feed. Keep the compost moist and stand the pot on damp gravel, but make sure the pot is not standing in water. After flowering the plants can be divided if necessary and put outside for the summer.

Phalaenopsis hybrids, moth orchids, have wonderful spikes of flowers in almost any colour you can imagine, often with contrasting spots or stripes. These orchids prefer warm conditions and, if kept warm, will continue to grow during the winter. The compost should be kept moist and the plants fed, although this needs to be done less frequently than in the summer. They also appreciate high humidity. Moth orchids should be watered all the year round, and they have no need of an autumn rest. If you are successful with them, you wisll find many thousands of other hybrids to tempt you and, once you have gained experience, you may like to try growing the orchid species in your conservatory.

Fig. 10.42 The attractive succulent *Aeonium arboreum* 'Schwarzkopf' can grow to a height of 2m (6½ft).

Fig. 10.43 The genus opuntia, the prickly pear, is well known to gardeners. While some can grow very large, others are suitable for the modest conservatory.

Fig. 10.44 Moth orchids flower throughout the year, but they need high temperatures to do well. This photograph shows the pink phalaenopsis 'Hennessy'.

Fig. 10.45 Cymbidium hybrids make superb conservatory plants. They are available in a wide range of colours, including red, white, pink and yellow. This is 'Saint Aubyn's Bay'.

143

GLOSSARY

ALI BABA A tall pot with a narrow neck which resembles the jars in which the thieves hid to attack 'Ali Baba'.

BRACTS Modified leaves surrounding a flower. They can be brightly coloured and look like petals as in bougainvillea.

BROMELIADS A family of plants which mainly originate from South America. The majority grow as epiphytes on trees or rocky cliffs, obtaining water and minerals from rainfall. The best known exception to this is the pineapple, which grows on the ground.

CHINOISERIE Describes any object, such as a jar, which is decorated in a Chinese style.

EPIPHYTES Plants which are not rooted in the ground but grow on another plant or on rocks. They are not parasitic – that is, they do not rely on the other plant for food or water but obtain minerals and water from rainfall.

ERICACEOUS Describes plants which belong to the heather family. These usually grow on acid soil, so compost for acid loving plants is described as ericaceous.

ESSENTIAL MINERALS These are the elements needed by a plant if it is to grow normally. Some, such as nitrogen, phosphorus and potassium are required in relatively large amounts, others in much lower concentrations or only as a trace element.

ÉTAGÈRE A stand with a number of shelves, one above another, for displaying plants.

FINIAL An ornament on the roof, pediment or gable of a conservatory.

FRONDS The compound leaf of a fern or cycad.

HABIT The overall shape or form of a plant. Whether it is upright, rounded or spreading.

HYBRIDS Plants produced by crossing two distinctly different parents. They can be different varieties, species or even genera.

JARDINIÈRE An ornamental stand for the display of plants.

OFFSHOOTS Shoot or branch that appears at the base of the main stem. These can sometimes be cut off and planted.

OGEE A gutter or other object moulded as a continuous double curve with the upper curve being convex and the lower concave.

PARASITES An animal or plant that lives on another and obtains all of its nourishment from the host.

PERLITE A naturally occurring volcanic rock which improves soil aeration and drainage.

PHOTOSYNTHESIS The process by which a green plant uses the energy of the sun to synthesize sugars and other compounds from carbon dioxide and water.

POT-BOUND The plant has filled the pot with roots and needs more compost to continue growing.

PREDATORS Carnivorous animals. In a horticultural context they prey on unwanted pests.

SEQUESTERONE A chemical which, when added to the soil or compost, makes iron available to the plant.

SERAMIS These special clay granules can be used instead of compost. They absorb water and release it gradually to the plant.

SLOW-RELEASE FERTILIZER A fertilizer, supplied in granular or tablet form, which releases the nutrients slowly over a whole growing season.

STAMENS Stamens are the male reproductive part of a flower which produce the pollen for fertilisation.

SYSTEMIC Describes a pesticide which moves up the plant from the point of contact so that any pest which attacks any part of the plant will be killed; in contrast to contact pesticides which only kill the pests that they come in contact with.

UNDERPLANTING When shade-loving plants are grown under tall plants it is called underplanting.

WATER STORAGE GRANULES Granules which, when added to the compost, retain water and release it slowly over a period of time.

VERMICULITE An inert heated-treated micaceous material which absorbs water and slowly releases it into the soil or compost.

ABOUT THE AUTHOR

After taking a degree in natural Sciences at Cambridge University, Joan Phelan worked for many years as an academic biologist. She had a particular interest in the relationships between the many cultivated members of thecabbage family and what influences their flavour and resistance to pests. Her research led to a Ph.D.

Ten years ago, after taking a course in garden design, she started Conservatory Gardens, a firm which aims to assist with every aspect of conservatories. It offers pre-building advice as well as help with choosing plants and how to care for them. Working as consultant has involved visiting a wide range of conservatories throughout the country and finding out what leads to success.
She has a large by London standards garden which runs down to the Thames. This was once described by a kind friend as a 'jungly garden'.

About twelve years ago a conservatory, designed by an architect, became a major interest. Since then she has identified how many changes she would have made to the design if she had started again. The conservatory houses a continually changing population of plants – it has been an ideal way to find out which species grow well and how best to care for them.

INDEX

Page numbers in bold refer to illustration captions

A SELECTION OF TITLES AVAILABLE FROM
GMC Publications
BOOKS

GARDENING

Alpine Gardening	Chris & Valerie Wheeler
Auriculas for Everyone: How to Grow and Show Perfect Plants	Mary Robinson
Beginners' Guide to Herb Gardening	Yvonne Cuthbertson
Beginners' Guide to Water Gardening	Graham Clarke
Big Leaves for Exotic Effect	Stephen Griffith
Companions to Clematis: Growing Clematis with Other Plants	Marigold Badcock
Creating Contrast with Dark Plants	Freya Martin
Creating Small Habitats for Wildlife in your Garden	Josie Briggs
Exotics are Easy	GMC Publications
Gardening with Hebes	Chris & Valerie Wheeler
Gardening with Shrubs	Eric Sawford
Gardening with Wild Plants	Julian Slatcher
Growing Cacti and Other Succulents in the Conservatory and Indoors	Shirley-Anne Bell
Growing Cacti and Other Succulents in the Garden	Shirley-Anne Bell
Growing Successful Orchids in the Greenhouse and Conservatory	Mark Isaac-Williams
Hardy Palms and Palm-Like Plants	Martyn Graham
Hardy Perennials: A Beginner's Guide	Eric Sawford
Hedges: Creating Screens and Edges	Averil Bedrich
How to Attract Butterflies to your Garden	John & Maureen Tampion
Marginal Plants	Bernard Sleeman
Orchids are Easy: A Beginner's Guide to their Care and Cultivation	Tom Gilland
Planting Plans for Your Garden	Jenny Shukman
Sink and Container Gardening Using Dwarf Hardy Plants	Chris & Valerie Wheeler
The Successful Conservatory and Growing Exotic Plants	Joan Phelan
Success with Bulbs	Eric Sawford
Success with Cuttings	Chris & Valerie Wheeler
Success with Seeds	Chris & Valerie Wheeler
Tropical Garden Style with Hardy Plants	Alan Hemsley
Water Garden Projects: From Groundwork to Planting	Roger Sweetinburgh

PHOTOGRAPHY

Close-Up on Insects	Robert Thompson
Digital Enhancement for Landscape Photographers	Arjan Hoogendam & Herb Parkin
Double Vision	Chris Weston & Nigel Hicks
An Essential Guide to Bird Photography	Steve Young
Field Guide to Bird Photography	Steve Young
Field Guide to Landscape Photography	Peter Watson
How to Photograph Pets	Nick Ridley
In my Mind's Eye: Seeing in Black and White	Charlie Waite
Life in the Wild: A Photographer's Year	Andy Rouse
Light in the Landscape: A Photographer's Year	Peter Watson
Photographers on Location with Charlie Waite	Charlie Waite
Photographing Wilderness	Jason Friend
Photographing your Garden	Gail Harland
Photography for the Naturalist	Mark Lucock
Photojournalism: An Essential Guide	David Herrod
Professional Landscape and Environmental Photography: From 35mm to Large Format	Mark Lucock
Rangefinder	Roger Hicks & Frances Schultz
Underwater Photography	Paul Kay
Where and How to Photograph Wildlife	Peter Evans
Wildlife Photography Workshops	Steve & Ann Toon

UPHOLSTERY

Upholstery: A Beginners' Guide	David James
Upholstery: A Complete Course (Revised Edition)	David James
Upholstery Restoration	David James
Upholstery Techniques & Projects	David James
Upholstery Tips and Hints	David James

CRAFTS

Bargello: A Fresh Approach to Florentine Embroidery	Brenda Day
Bead and Sequin Embroidery Stitches	Stanley Levy
Beginning Picture Marquetry	Lawrence Threadgold
Blackwork: A New Approach	Brenda Day
Celtic Backstitch	Helen Hall
Celtic Cross Stitch Designs	Carol Phillipson
Celtic Knotwork Designs	Sheila Sturrock
Celtic Knotwork Handbook	Sheila Sturrock
Celtic Spirals and Other Designs	Sheila Sturrock
Celtic Spirals Handbook	Sheila Sturrock
Complete Pyrography	Stephen Poole
Creating Made-to-Measure Knitwear: A Revolutionary Approach to Knitwear Design	Sylvia Wynn
Creative Backstitch	Helen Hall
Creative Log-Cabin Patchwork	Pauline Brown
Creative Machine Knitting	GMC Publications
Cross-Stitch Designs from China	Carol Phillipson
Cross-Stitch Designs from India	Carol Phillipson
Cross-Stitch Floral Designs	Joanne Sanderson
Cross-Stitch Gardening Projects	Joanne Sanderson
Decoration on Fabric: A Sourcebook of Ideas	Pauline Brown
Decorative Beaded Purses	Enid Taylor
Designing and Making Cards	Glennis Gilruth
Designs for Pyrography and Other Crafts	Norma Gregory
Dried Flowers: A Complete Guide	Lindy Bird
Easy Wedding Planner	Jenny Hopkin
Exotic Textiles in Needlepoint	Stella Knight
Glass Engraving Pattern Book	John Everett
Glass Painting	Emma Sedman
Handcrafted Rugs	Sandra Hardy
Hand-Dyed Yarn Craft Projects	Debbie Tomkies
Hobby Ceramics: Techniques and Projects for Beginners	Patricia A. Waller
How to Arrange Flowers: A Japanese Approach to English Design	Taeko Marvelly
How to Make First-Class Cards	Debbie Brown
An Introduction to Crewel Embroidery	Mave Glenny
Machine-Knitted Babywear	Christine Eames
Making Fabergé-Style Eggs	Denise Hopper
Making Fairies and Fantastical Creatures	Julie Sharp
Making Hand-Sewn Boxes: Techniques and Projects	Jackie Woolsey
Making Kumihimo: Japanese Interlaced Braids	Rodrick Owen
Making Mini Cards, Gift Tags & Invitations	Glennis Gilruth
Making Polymer Clay Cards and Tags	Jacqui Eccleson
Making Wirecraft Cards	Kate MacFadyen
Native American Bead Weaving	Lynne Garner
New Ideas for Crochet: Stylish Projects for the Home	Darsha Capaldi
Paddington Bear in Cross-Stitch	Leslie Hills
Papercraft Projects for Special Occasions	Sine Chesterman
Papermaking and Bookbinding: Coastal Inspirations	Joanne Kaar

153

Patchwork for Beginners	*Pauline Brown*
Pyrography Designs	*Norma Gregory*
Rose Windows for Quilters	*Angela Besley*
Silk Painting for Beginners	*Jill Clay*
Sponge Painting	*Ann Rooney*
Stained Glass: Techniques and Projects	*Mary Shanahan*
Step-by-Step Card Making	*Glennis Gilruth*
Step-by-Step Pyrography Projects for the Solid Point Machine	*Norma Gregory*
Stitched Cards and Gift Tags for Special Occasions	*Carol Phillipson*
Tassel Making for Beginners	*Enid Taylor*
Tatting Collage	*Lindsay Rogers*
Tatting Patterns	*Lyn Morton*
Temari: A Traditional Japanese Embroidery Technique	*Margaret Ludlow*
Three-Dimensional Découpage: Innovative Projects for Beginners	*Hilda Stokes*
Trompe l'Oeil: Techniques and Projects	*Jan Lee Johnson*
Tudor Treasures to Embroider	*Pamela Warner*
Wax Art	*Hazel Marsh*

WOODCARVING

Beginning Woodcarving	*GMC Publications*
Carving Architectural Detail in Wood: The Classical Tradition	*Frederick Wilbur*
Carving Birds & Beasts	*GMC Publications*
Carving Classical Styles in Wood	*Frederick Wilbur*
Carving the Human Figure: Studies in Wood and Stone	*Dick Onians*
Carving Nature: Wildlife Studies in Wood	*Frank Fox-Wilson*
Celtic Carved Lovespoons: 30 Patterns	*Sharon Littley & Clive Griffin*
Decorative Woodcarving (New Edition)	*Jeremy Williams*
Elements of Woodcarving	*Chris Pye*

Figure Carving in Wood: Human and Animal Forms	*Sara Wilkinson*
Lettercarving in Wood: A Practical Course	*Chris Pye*
Relief Carving in Wood: A Practical Introduction	*Chris Pye*
Woodcarving for Beginners	*GMC Publications*
Woodcarving Made Easy	*Cynthia Rogers*
Woodcarving Tools, Materials & Equipment (New Edition in 2 vols.)	*Chris Pye*

VIDEOS

Drop-in and Pinstuffed Seats	*David James*
Stuffover Upholstery	*David James*
Elliptical Turning	*David Springett*
Woodturning Wizardry	*David Springett*
Turning Between Centres: The Basics	*Dennis White*
Turning Bowls	*Dennis White*
Boxes, Goblets and Screw Threads	*Dennis White*
Novelties and Projects	*Dennis White*
Classic Profiles	*Dennis White*
Twists and Advanced Turning	*Dennis White*
Sharpening the Professional Way	*Jim Kingshott*
Sharpening Turning & Carving Tools	*Jim Kingshott*
Bowl Turning	*John Jordan*
Hollow Turning	*John Jordan*
Woodturning: A Foundation Course	*Keith Rowley*
Carving a Figure: The Female Form	*Ray Gonzalez*
The Router: A Beginner's Guide	*Alan Goodsell*
The Scroll Saw: A Beginner's Guide	*John Burke*

MAGAZINES

Woodturning ◆ Woodcarving ◆ Furniture & Cabinetmaking
The Router ◆ New Woodworking ◆ The Dolls' House Magazine
Outdoor Photography ◆ Black & White Photography
Knitting ◆ Guild News

The above represents a full list of all titles currently published or scheduled to be published.
All are available direct from the Publishers or through bookshops, newsagents and specialist retailers.
To place an order, or to obtain a complete catalogue, contact:

GMC Publications,
Castle Place, 166 High Street, Lewes, East Sussex BN7 1XU United Kingdom
Tel: 01273 488005 Fax: 01273 402866
E-mail: pubs@thegmcgroup.com
Website: www.gmcbooks.com

Orders by credit card are accepted